345.73
T

Trespacz, Karen L.

The trial of
gangster Al Capone :
a headline court
case

$18.86

DATE DUE	BORROWER'S NAME	ROOM NO

345.73
T

Trespacz, Karen L.

The trial of
gangster Al Capone :
a headline court
case

804278 01886   36240B

THE TRIAL
OF GANGSTER
AL CAPONE

A Headline Court Case

Headline Court Cases

The Trial of Gangster Al Capone
A Headline Court Case
0-7660-1482-7

The Alger Hiss Communist Spy Trial
A Headline Court Case
0-7660-1483-5

The Andersonville Prison Civil War Crimes Trial
A Headline Court Case
0-7660-1386-3

The Court-Martial Trial of West Point Cadet Johnson Whittaker
A Headline Court Case
0-7660-1485-1

The John Brown Slavery Revolt Trial
A Headline Court Case
0-7660-1385-5

The Lindbergh Baby Kidnapping Trial
A Headline Court Case
0-7660-1389-8

The Lizzie Borden "Axe Murder" Trial
A Headline Court Case
0-7660-1422-3

The Mary Surratt "Lincoln Assassination" Trial
A Headline Court Case
0-7660-1481-9

The Nuremberg Nazi War Crimes Trials
A Headline Court Case
0-7660-1384-7

The O. J. Simpson Murder Trial
A Headline Court Case
0-7660-1480-0

The Rosenberg Cold War Spy Trial
A Headline Court Case
0-7660-1479-7

The Sacco and Vanzetti Controversial Murder Trial
A Headline Court Case
0-7660-1387-1

The Salem Witchcraft Trials
A Headline Court Case
0-7660-1383-9

The Scopes Monkey Trial
A Headline Court Case
0-7660-1338-X

The Teapot Dome Scandal Trial
A Headline Court Case
0-7660-1484-3

THE TRIAL
OF GANGSTER
AL CAPONE

A Headline Court Case

Karen L. Trespacz

Enslow Publishers, Inc.

40 Industrial Road   PO Box 38
Box 398   Aldershot
Berkeley Heights, NJ 07922   Hants GU12 6BP
USA   UK

http://www.enslow.com

Library of Congress Cataloging-in-Publication Data

Trespacz, Karen L.
  The trial of gangster Al Capone: a headline court case / Karen
Trespacz.
    p. cm. — (Headline court cases)
Includes bibliographical references and index.
  ISBN 0-7660-1482-7
  1. Capone, Al, 1899-1947—Trials, litigation, etc.—Juvenile
literature. 2. Trials (Tax evasion)—Illinois—Chicago—Juvenile
literature. I. Title. II. Series.
  KF224.C355 T74 2001
  345.73'0233—dc21

                          00-012168

Printed in the United States of America

10 9 8 7 6 5 4 3 2

To Our Readers:
We have done our best to make sure all Internet addresses in this book were active and
appropriate when we went to press. However, the author and the publisher have no
control over and assume no liability for the material available on those Internet sites or on
other Web sites they may link to. Any comments or suggestions can be sent by e-mail to
comments@enslow.com or to the address on the back cover.

Contents

chapter one

MASSACRE

CHICAGO, ILLINOIS— The dog would not stop howling. Its frantic, insistent sound carried across the street, piercing through the doors and windows shut tight against the freezing cold of that February morning in Chicago in 1929.

The German shepherd's desperate wailing carried all the way through to Mrs. Max Landesman, who was ironing in her apartment across the street. It called to her that something was wrong, terribly wrong.[1] So she convinced Charles McAllister, her boarder, who was about to leave for work, to go over to 2122 North Clark Street to see what the problem was.

McAllister broke through the door, went in, and came right back out again, shaking. His face was white with shock. He had just seen a sight that would unnerve even those experienced with gang violence.[2] Based on the only words the almost speechless McAllister could manage—"They're all dead!"—Mrs. Landesman phoned the police station.[3]

The blood splattered over the walls and running across the concrete floor was still warm. But the events leading up to the horror in the garage started with cold-blooded scheming. First, the killers had to figure out how to get the victims to hold still. If the victims realized they were about to be gunned down, they would be very likely to start shooting back. How much simpler the task of killing them would be if they would peacefully give up their guns and turn around with their hands in the air. That would never happen if they thought they were being approached by hitmen, hired killers.

But if the victims thought the men with guns were *police*, well, that would be a different story. Gangsters made so many payments to Chicago police in those days that the police generally did not hurt them. Gangsters were arrested, sure. Police took them to the police station for questioning. But the police did not kill gangsters. So when police announced a raid, gangsters usually felt safe enough to put down their weapons and follow the instructions to turn around. Stolen police uniforms would let the assassins do their murdering at point-blank range without much chance of getting hurt themselves.

But the disguises would not work unless the doomed gangsters could be tricked into being at the right place at the right time. So the schemers used a load of stolen whiskey as bait to lure the victims into the trap. A bootlegger, someone who made, bought, and/or sold alcohol illegally, had sold the gangsters a shipment once before and everything went smoothly. So, there was no reason for George "Bugs" Moran, the target of this careful plotting, to be suspicious when the hijacker called to offer him another shipment. They set the day (tomorrow), time (10:30 A.M.) and place (2122 North Clark Street, the site of the gang's garage-turned-warehouse) for the bootlegger to deliver the whiskey.

The date they set was not just any date. It was February 14. The plan called for Moran to get a special Valentine's Day present that day—not the whiskey he was expecting, but a bouquet of bullets.

The plan worked almost perfectly. Two lookouts—brothers—had rented a room across the street so they could watch the gangsters arrive. They saw various men arrive at the garage, getting ready to meet the bootlegger's truck. One man brought his German shepherd, Highball. Most of the men were gangsters, but one was not. Young optometrist (eye doctor) Reinhardt H. Schwimmer thought gangsters were cool and he liked to hang out with them.[4]

When the lookouts saw a man who looked just like Moran—large, heavy, wearing a gray overcoat and a tan felt hat with a brim—they called in the signal. By the time the stolen police car pulled up outside 2122 North Clark, there were seven men inside the garage.

But here is where the glitch occurred in the "perfect" plot. The lookouts thought they had seen Moran. But the lookouts had been brought in from Detroit so as not to raise suspicions.[5] They were not really familiar with Moran. The person who triggered their signal was not Moran but Al

Weinshank, a man who looked a lot like Moran and who happened to dress like him that day. The real Moran came around the corner just as the police car pulled up. Seeing the police uniforms, Moran took off.

Four men from the police car, two in uniform, went into the garage; leaving the driver in the car. Inside, the slaughter took place according to plan. Weapons were turned over to the "police," the gangsters lined up facing the back wall, and by the time the two men holding machine guns opened fire it was too late. Almost all of the victims died in minutes—including Schwimmer. The only man not to die at the scene died in a hospital about three hours later.

Their work done, the four hitmen marched out. The two dressed in street clothes went first with their hands up. The two dressed in police uniforms came behind, weapons pointed at their backs. They tried to make it look as though police had the first men under arrest, just in case someone had heard the gunfire and looked out the window. "No need to be alarmed," they tried to make the scene say. "Everything is under control. You can go back to whatever it was you were doing and forget all about this."

But Chicago could not forget about it; the nation could not forget about it. It was too horrible. Who could have done this? Moran pointed the finger saying, "Only Capone kills like that."[6]

Moran did not even have to say the first name; everyone knew he meant Al Capone, the most powerful gangster in Chicago.

Chicago had already seen Capone's guns attack. On

August 10, 1926, several Capone gunmen started firing at two rival gangsters in front of the Standard Oil Building on a busy weekday morning. The attacked gangsters started shooting back. Innocent passersby ran, ducked, and hid trying to escape the bullets, but one of them was shot in the thigh. When the police arrived, one of the targeted gangsters, Vincent "Schemer" Drucci, jumped into a nearby car, pointed his gun at the driver's head and barked, "Take me away and make it snappy!"[7] The police grabbed Drucci before the car was out of reach. As if that incident were not enough, the Capone gang did it again—at the same busy place, with the same rival gangsters—five days later.

The danger to the public was not just in attacks *by* Capone but also in attacks *on* Capone. One of those attacks on Capone happened on September 20, 1926, in Cicero, a Chicago suburb that served as Capone's headquarters. There were more people out and about than usual that day because tourists had come to see the races at the nearby Hawthorne Racetrack.

Al Capone and his bodyguard, Frankie Rio, were having coffee after lunch in the back of the Hawthorne Inn restaurant, watching the crowds. Suddenly the terrible sound of a machine gun came from a car driving down the busy street out front. Then just as suddenly as the racket started, it stopped.

Capone got up and started walking toward the front of the restaurant to check it out. But something did not seem right to Rio; there was no shattered glass. Then he realized—the gun had been shooting blanks, fake bullets. It was bait to lure Capone out into the open. Rio jumped to his feet and tackled Capone before he could make it to the door. "It's a stall, boss!" Rio warned. "The real stuff hasn't started. You stay down!"

Rio was right. Just a few moments later, the real shooting started. It came from a long line of slow-moving black limousines one block behind the "attention" car. The limousines' windows were filled with machine-gun barrels. The gunfire hit the Hawthorne Hotel, the Anton Hotel, storefronts, and cars parked on that side of the street. Windows were shattered. People screamed. Bullets chewed into buildings and splintered their wooden trimmings.

The deadly parade pulled up in front of the Hawthorne Inn and the firing stopped while a man wearing brown over-alls and a khaki shirt got out of the second to last car. He casually walked over to the door of the restaurant. At the door, he knelt. With his machine gun set on rapid-fire, he emptied a 100-round cartridge of bullets deep into the restaurant. When he was finished, he strolled back to one of the waiting cars. A driver gave the three-honk signal, and the black procession moved off down the street. (This was how *Moran* killed. He invented the bullet-spewing motorcade.[8])

Amazingly, the most serious damage done in that attack came not from bullets but from flying glass. Mrs. Anna Freeman had come from Louisiana to see the races with her husband and their five-year-old son. The three of them were caught in their car when the firestorm started. Afterward, Mr. Freeman found a bullet hole in his hat. Their son had a bullet hole in his jacket and blood trickling across his knee.

Police raided a gamblers' den in Chicago in 1925 and several loads of gamblers were taken into custody.

Anna Freeman had a piece of their exploded windshield in her right eye; it took special surgery to save her eyesight.

Only one other person was hurt in that blizzard of a thousand bullets—a Capone gunman walking into the restaurant when the firing started was hit in the shoulder.

Not everything was property damage and close calls; there were murders, too, hundreds of them. (Capone was said to have ordered several hundred murders himself.) In 1925 alone, the city of Chicago experienced more than one hundred bombings.[9] Yet, little was being done to stop these things. Part of the reason for the lack of action was the money gangsters paid to people who should have been doing something. Part of the reason was fear.

Take, for example, the time Capone shot and killed Joe

Howard in front of three people. Right after the murder, witnesses said it was Capone, but when the time came to testify, the witnesses all had a different story. One witness said he could not see what happened, the second said he could not identify the killer, and the third witness could not be found at all.

It almost seemed like nothing *could* be done to stop the violence. But with the St. Valentine's Day Massacre shocking the nation, the new president of the United States, Herbert Hoover, gave the order to "get" Capone.[10]

But how? Capone and his organization had been involved in murder and a lot of illegal activities—gambling, prostitution, and (since alcoholic beverages were illegal in those days) selling booze. Nobody had been able to put Capone in jail for any of those things, even though everyone knew he was doing them.

Then somebody came up with an idea. It was crazy, but it was so crazy it just might work. Al Capone ignored a lot of laws, including the federal income tax law. Federal income tax is an amount of money paid to the federal government each year based on how much money a person makes. What was the penalty for deliberately not paying federal income tax? Going to jail—right where officials wanted him.

So the federal government started putting together a case they could take to court. They would not claim that Al Capone was a murderer. They would not say that Al Capone was masterminding an immense organization of illegal activities. They would maintain instead that Al Capone had knowingly and willfully not paid his federal income taxes for many years.

chapter 2

AL CAPONE

BORN IN AMERICA—Al Capone's parents, Gabriel and Teresa Capone, came to New York City from Naples, Italy, in the early 1890s. Al's oldest brother, Vincenzo, had been born in Italy and came with them; accounts differ as to whether the next son, Raffaele, was born in the United States or in Italy before coming to the United States as a baby. Al and the rest of his brothers and sisters were born in New York.

Al had six brothers and two sisters. They each had their given names, but the boys became known by "American" names, too. The Capone children were:

- Vincenzo, born 1892, who was called James.

- Raffaele, born January 12, 1894, who became Ralph.

- Salavatore, born January 1895, called Frank.

- Alphonse, born January 17, 1899, or "Al" Capone.

- Amadeo Ermino, born 1901. His American name was John but the family called him Mimi.

- Umberto, born 1906, who became Albert John.

- Matthew Nicholas, born 1908, known as Matt.

- Rosalia, born 1910, called Rose. She is thought to have died when still a baby.

- Mafalda, born January 28, 1912, who was named after an Italian princess and was never known by any other name.[1]

The Capone family was poor, starting out their American life in an apartment in the section of Brooklyn, New York, where many Italian immigrants settled. None of the apartments there had bathrooms. The only hot water was water they heated themselves on their only source of heat, a potbellied coal stove. But they were a little better off than most Italian immigrants were. Gabriel was a barber and had started a barbershop not far from their apartment.

Gabriel took to his new American life, and in 1906 he became an American citizen.[2] (This event may have made a big impression on seven-year-old Al. When he grew up, Al did not refer to himself as Italian; he always said he was American.) Teresa became an American citizen automatically when her husband did. All throughout Al's life, though, his mother continued to speak Italian.

Al started school at P.S. 7 in 1904 at age five. His sixteen-year-old teacher, Sadie, remembered him as being big and strong for his age, with a quick temper. The other boys would pick on him because his nose dripped during the winter. The Irish boys nicknamed him "Macaroni."[3] He went to a different public school starting in second grade. He got

This family is coming to the United States from Italy about fifteen years after Al Capone's family did. This picture was taken at Ellis Island, the first landing place for many immigrants.

B's all through school until sixth grade. Then, his math and English grades dropped, mostly because he missed school so much.

Not many students went all the way through high school in those days. High school was new then; New York City had only started offering high school education in 1897. Then, too, since the average Italian earned only around $10.50 a week, family members were expected to leave school and start earning money as soon as they could.[4] (The only Capone brother to go all the way through high school was the youngest, Matt.) The oldest brother, Vincenzo, did not just leave school, he left the state. He ran away from home in 1908, when he was sixteen, to join the circus.

Because of his poor grades, Al had to repeat sixth grade. It must have been embarrassing, and one day when his teacher gave him a talking to, he sassed her in return. So she hit him and he hit her back. She took him to the principal, who beat him up. Al never went back to school again.

Out on the streets at age fourteen, Al came to know Johnny Torrio, the adult leader of the Five Pointers gang. This gang was so bad that when Theodore Roosevelt was New York City's Police Commissioner, he said the Five Pointers were "the biggest threat to decency and respect for law in any part of our city."[5]

But Johnny Torrio did not take on just any unschooled kid; Al had to pass a test. Torrio told Al to come see him at a certain time. When Al showed up, he did not find Torrio, but he did find a pile of money. Unlike most of the people Torrio tested, Al did not take any of the money. That was how Torrio knew Al was trustworthy and worth trying out on bigger jobs.[6]

One of the jobs Torrio arranged for eighteen-year-old Al was as a bouncer and bartender. (A bouncer is someone who convinces people to leave a bar if they are getting too rowdy.) One summer night, Frank Galluccio came into the place where Al worked. Galluccio had brought a date and his younger sister, Lena. Al could not take his eyes off Lena and kept coming by to talk to her, even though she did not want anything to do with him.

Galluccio tried to protect his sister from Capone. Galluccio took out his four-inch knife and lunged for Capone's throat. His missed, but not by much. Galluccio carved three big gashes on the left side of Al Capone's jaw; one of them ran down his neck under his left ear. It took thirty stitches to close the wounds. The injuries left three white scars—and Al Capone would become famous in newspapers around the world as "Scarface" Capone. (Some people might wear scars as a badge of honor, but not Al Capone. For a long time, he would cover the left side of his face if he saw a camera, and he often wore heavy powder to hide the scars.)

The following year, in 1918, nineteen-year-old Al Capone fell in love, got married, and became a father. The woman who stole his heart was Mae Coughlin. Tall, blond, and Irish, she was two years older than he was. When they registered for their marriage certificate, he added a year and she subtracted one to make it look like they were the same age. They named their son—their only child—Albert Francis Capone, but always called him "Sonny."

Meanwhile Torrio was called out to Chicago to help a relative, "Big Jim" Colosimo, who was having trouble with the Black Hand. The Black Hand was not really a gang, it was a method of scaring people out of their money (the legal word for this is "extortion"). One Black Hand letter went like this:

> You got some cash. I need $1,000.00. You place the $100.00 bills in an envelope and place it underneath a board at the northeast corner of Sixty-ninth and Euclid at eleven o'clock tonight. If you place the money there you will live. If you don't you die. If you report this to the police, I'll kill you when I get out. . . .[7]

Torrio solved Big Jim's problem. He lured the three men who were threatening Torrio into an ambush and had them gunned down. That not only stopped those three, but also scared other people who might have tried it.

Colosimo convinced Torrio to stay in Chicago and

become a part of Colosimo's organization. In addition to the illegal activities, the organization also included a famous nightclub, Colosimo's Café, which was *the* place to go.

But Colosimo's empire did not include bootlegging (making, moving, and selling illegal liquor). Colosimo's businesses would sell liquor to patrons, of course, but that was only a few hundred people. Torrio realized that a lot more money could be made distributing booze to drinking places all over Chicago—that would be selling to thousands and maybe even hundreds of thousands of people.

But Big Jim was not interested. Why should he be? He liked what he was doing. He had a name for himself. Big Jim had plenty of money already. He wore diamonds everywhere—on his belt, on his suspenders, on his vest, and on every finger. He even carried loose diamonds in his pocket the way other people carried pennies and

This picture was taken of Al Capone the same year that he became head of Johnny Torrio's crime organization in Chicago. Capone was twenty-six years old.

paperclips. If he was feeling generous, he would sometimes hand out a diamond as a gift.

Then, even though Big Jim had been married for a number of years, he fell in love with a young singer in his café, Dale Winter. He was so in love that he started ignoring the business to devote all his attention to Winter. He divorced his wife and only three weeks later married Winter, explaining to a friend that "This is the real thing."[8]

It was too much for Torrio, a man devoted to both his business and his wife. Big Jim was making three big mistakes. He was passing up a golden opportunity by not bootlegging. He was neglecting the business. And worst of all, he had broken up his family over a crush on a younger woman.

So Torrio made arrangements to have Big Jim killed. Somebody made an appointment to meet Big Jim at Colosimo's Café around 4 P.M. on May 11, 1920, about a week after Big Jim got back from his honeymoon. That someone never showed up, but a gunman did. As Big Jim walked through the café to the street to see if his appointment was coming, the gunman came out of a coatroom and shot and killed Colosimo.

Torrio was now head of Colosimo's organization. To expand into the new bootlegging business, he needed help. Torrio called Capone.

It is not entirely clear when and how Capone fit into Torrio's bloody takeover. There are those who say that Capone did not come to Chicago until after Colosimo was dead. There are those who say he was there well before that, and may have helped Torrio arrange the murder. There are even those who are convinced that Capone was the gunman in the coatroom. But whenever Capone did come, he made Chicago his new home.

Six months after Torrio became head of the organization, Capone became head of his extended family. On November 20, 1920, his father went to a pool hall in New York where he and Al had spent hours playing pool when Al was a boy. It was there that Gabriel Capone's bad heart gave out and he collapsed watching others play. Friends carried Gabriel back to his apartment where he died before the doctor could get there.

Capone went to New York for the funeral, and then made plans to bring his mother and siblings to Chicago. (He eventually brought his father's body to Chicago, too, and had it buried at Mount Olivet Cemetery.) Capone bought some property in a quiet residential neighborhood and had a large brick house built.

The house at 7244 South Prairie was big enough for most of his family to live with him. His brother Ralph with his wife and two children lived on the top floor. Capone lived on the bottom floor with his wife and son, his mother, and his sister Mafalda. Various other brothers and cousins lived there from time to time, too. And one by one, Capone took care of his extended family by finding them jobs, usually within the "outfit," as the illegal organization was called.

Capone himself, meanwhile, continued to advance in his chosen "profession." In fact, when the Chicago Crime

The tall house is the Chicago home where Al Capone brought his family after his father died. Capone's mother continued to live here even after Capone, his wife, and their son moved to a house near Miami, Florida.

Commission published its first list of "Public Enemies," Al Capone was right at the top—becoming the country's first "Public Enemy Number One." But he was still working for Johnny Torrio. And he might have stayed second fiddle to Torrio if not for one thing—revenge.

On November 10, 1924, Torrio and Capone's organization had killed Dion O'Banion after he had doublecrossed them in a deal. Some of O'Banion's associates—including Bugs Moran, Schemer Drucci, and Hymie Weiss—decided to kill Torrio in revenge for O'Banion's death.

So on January 24, 1925, as Johnny Torrio and his wife, Ann, returned to their apartment after a shopping trip, Torrio was ambushed. Right in front of his horrified wife, Moran and Weiss leaped out of a car and started firing at Torrio, covering his body with bullets. Moran stood over Torrio's bleeding body, put his gun to Torrio's forehead, and pulled the trigger for the final shot into his brain—but discovered he had run out of bullets. Moran started to reload his gun, but a laundry truck came around the corner. Drucci honked the "let's get out of here" signal, and they all took off.

Ann Torrio grabbed her husband's blasted body by the shoulders and dragged him over the icy sidewalk into the apartment building. A neighbor across the street called the police and an ambulance took Torrio, barely alive, to the hospital.

Capone came over to the hospital as soon as he heard what happened. Although two police officers were stationed to guard the patient, Capone assigned several more gunmen from the outfit to protect Torrio. Capone slept in the hospital near his boss until Torrio was well enough to be released.

Torrio decided enough was enough. He met with Capone, perhaps in March 1925, and turned over leadership of the outfit to him. So at age twenty-six, Al Capone became the head of the largest crime organization in Chicago.

It was estimated that by 1927, Capone's organization made about $105 million—an impressive figure now, an overwhelming figure then. The income came from a variety of illegal sources:

Alcohol manufacture and sale	$60 million
Gambling	$25 million
Corruption and resort	$10 million
Other rackets	$10 million[9]

Capone also put together a fearsome team to help run the organization. His brother Ralph (known as "Bottles" Capone) handled liquor sales. Jake "Greasy Thumb" Guzik was the business manager. And Frank Nitti was "The Enforcer." A gang member explained Nitti's role to an undercover federal agent:

> . . . When the guys from out of town louse up a job and only "hurt" somebody, The Enforcer don't fool around none. He has one of his own guys get the two guys who blew the job. That's why very few fellows get hurt around here. They get kilt [sic].[10]

Unlike other gangs, Capone picked men for ability, not on the basis of nationality. A news photographer who knew Capone observed: "He knew how to pick people for certain positions in certain categories. . . . He had people of every nationality you could think of: Irish, Swedes, Poles, Germans, and Jews. . . ."[11]

This appreciation for ability also included African Americans. Milt Hinton, a black bass player, maintained that Capone was "the only white gangster in Chicago who gave black musicians a fair shake."[12]

Capone often had canvas sacks stuffed with cash lying around his office. And he was not reluctant to spend it on himself. He had very expensive suits made especially for him (the right-hand pockets were made extra strong so they could carry a gun without ripping). He wore a platinum watch chain that sparkled with diamonds and a huge, flawless blue-white diamond ring.

But he did not spend money only on himself. He was known for his generosity. He used to spend $100,000 on Christmas presents for each of his friends and family members.[13] He sent his sister, Mafalda, to a private girls' school and every year he would play Santa Claus, passing out presents to all the students and teachers. He liked to give out belt buckles to friends with their initials spelled out in diamonds; he once placed an order for thirty buckles.

He also helped people pay for the necessities of life. The lowest positions in his organization paid $100 to $500 a week, at a time when a woman store clerk might earn $6.50 a week.[14] Capone even hired Frank Galluccio, the man who gave him the scars, at $100 a week.

His generosity was not limited to those who worked for him. One story tells of the time he helped an old woman who had been thrown into the street because she could not pay her rent. Capone told his men to gather up all her things—*carefully*, so nothing was damaged—and settle her into an apartment that Capone paid for. Cicero shopkeepers had instructions to give food and clothes to the poor—and to give them fuel during winter—and Capone would pay for it. As one person who was a teenager during those years said, "If people were desperate and needed help, he was there to help them. . . . [A]nd he never expected you to pay him back."[15]

Capone also became very powerful in Chicago. Perhaps the most vivid example of his power occurred during the election of 1928. Frank Loesch, president of the Chicago Crime Commission, was very worried about the national elections coming up in the fall. There had been so much bombing during the primary elections in the spring that the elections were known as the "Pineapple Primary." (Gangsters' homemade bombs were called "pineapples.")

The police had not been able to do anything, so Loesch did the unthinkable. Toward the end of August, this "tall, straight, white-haired but vigorous" seventy-six-year-old head of the Chicago Crime Commission went to see a twenty-nine-year-old gangster. They met at Capone's main office in the Lexington Hotel. After an introductory chat, Loesch bravely got down to business: "I am here to ask you to help in one thing. I want you to keep your . . . hoodlums out of the election this coming fall."[16]

It is not a good idea to insult someone you want favors from, but Capone considered the request anyway.

Loesch was amazed. He had not really expected Capone to be helpful. Yet, Capone was offering to take care of his own gang and others, too.

It was an offer Loesch could not pass up. Sure, he would be very grateful for the help, he said. Capone's answer was even more of a surprise: "All right," said Capone. "I'll have the cops send over squad cars the night before the election and jug [arrest] all the hoodlums and keep 'em in the cooler [jail] until the polls close."[17]

They shook hands on it, leaving Loesch to marvel that a

gangster was calmly promising to mobilize the police—the *police*—in a way that nobody else, certainly nobody legal, could.

The evening before the election, the police rounded up many known hoodlums, and put them in jail until after the elections. On the day of the elections, seventy police cars roamed the streets. As Loesch said later: "It turned out to be the most successful election day that Chicago had in forty years. There was not one complaint, not one election fraud, not one threat of trouble all day."[18] ·

But even though Al Capone had a great deal of power he also had problems. Take, for example, the May 16, 1925, raid on one of Capone's primary gambling spots, the Hawthorne Smoke Shop in Cicero. Henry C. Hoover, a young minister from a nearby town, led the raid.

The raid started a bit after noon, when Capone was still asleep. (Capone was noted for sleeping at least until noon, because he was also noted for partying until very late at night.) The Smoke Shop was across the street from the Hawthorne Hotel where Capone was staying. Hearing the commotion, Capone pulled on some pants and came across the street.

He pushed past the raiders milling around inside, went to the back office, and starting jamming money into his pockets. There was too much of it, so Capone had his cousin, Charley Fischetti, help bring cash across the street to the hotel.

Capone returned dressed up and tried to reason with Hoover. "Can't you and I get together," he asked. "Come to an understanding?"[19] Capone then offered to stay out of the minister's town if the minister left Capone alone in Cicero. The minister was not about to make peace with sin, so Capone switched gears. His men broke Charles Bragg's nose and beat up another raider, David Morgan. Later, Morgan was shot and left to die. They did not try raiding again.

Having all this money and power did not mean that Capone felt safe—far from it. On January 12, 1925, Bugs Moran, Hymie Weiss, and Schemer Drucci destroyed Capone's car in a drive-by shooting that badly hurt Capone's driver and sent Capone's cousin Charley diving for the floor. Although Capone was not in the car at the time, the event shook him up so much that he had a special car made. It was armor-plated and had bulletproof glass. It even had special combination locks to make it harder for enemies to plant bombs inside. The average Cadillac at the time weighed about two tons. Capone's Cadillac weighed seven tons.

Despite Capone's best efforts to protect himself, the attempts to kill him continued. In the year and a half after O'Banion's death, men from O'Banion's gang tried to kill Capone about a dozen times.[20] A couple of years later, another group (which also included Moran) promised to pay fifty thousand dollars to whoever killed Capone. For about six months, killers came from all over the country to try to earn the money.

So Capone had a scout car go in front of his reinforced Cadillac and a car loaded with gunmen drove behind it. Whenever he went anywhere, it was usually in the middle of a pack of bodyguards, and he had bodyguards patrol four square blocks around wherever he was. For several years, one of his bodyguards slept outside of his bedroom, guns in hand. The chef at his headquarters tasted everything Capone ate or drank to make sure it was not poisoned. (Rivals once tried to pay the cook at one of Capone's favorite restaurants ten thousand dollars to slip some acid into Capone's soup.)[21]

Capone's security measures were greater than those used at the time to protect the president of the United States. Even so, in that casual chat with Loesch before they got down to business, Capone told Loesch that he expected he would die at the hands of a killer.[22]

Nor could Capone protect the people close to him. His brother Frank died in a swarm of bullets from a police convoy in the spring of 1924. One of Capone's drivers, Tommy, disappeared. Two boys, aged thirteen and eleven, who had led their horse to water, found him. When the horse would not drink, the boys poked around in the water. That was where they found Tommy's body.

In fact, Capone lost people close to him *because* they were close to him. In one three-month period, fifteen people close to him were murdered.[23]

Perhaps because of this danger to himself and people he cared about, Capone was known for trying to make peace before he went to war. In October 1926, when gang murders were running about twelve a month, he got Chicago's gangsters together at the Hotel Sherman to convince them to solve conflicts peacefully. All the bootleg murders did stop for a little over two months afterward. As Capone said:

"They stay on the North Side and I stay in Cicero and if we meet on the street, we say 'hello' and shake hands. . . ."[24]

Capone even tried for peace after the Hawthorne Inn shoot-up described in the first chapter. But instead of producing peace, these negotiations highlighted another of Capone's virtues—loyalty. Hymie Weiss said the only way Capone could buy his own safety would be to turn over two of his men, Albert Anselmi and John Scalise, for certain death. Capone replied heatedly, "I wouldn't do that to a yellow dog!" and the peace talks were over.[25]

Al Capone did not like being known as a thug. He complained:

> I've had to do a lot of things I don't like to do. But I'm not as [bad] as I'm painted. I'm human. I've got a heart in me. I'll go as deep in my pocket as any man to help a guy that needs help. I can't stand to see anybody hungry or cold or helpless. . . . I don't take any credit to myself for being charitable and I'm just saying this to show that I'm not the worst man in the world.[26]

He also disliked the bad publicity because of "the hurt it brings to my mother and my family. They hear so much about what a terrible criminal I am. It's getting too much for them and I'm sick of it all myself."[27]

His sister Mafalda also complained about the unflattering news stories, "I wish they would say how good he is. Everyone who really knows him says it."[28]

But if he was that kind-hearted, what about the murders? A newspaper reporter once asked him what a gangster thought about when he murdered somebody. Capone replied:

Well, maybe he thinks that the law of self-defense, the way God looks at it, is a little broader than the law books have it. Maybe it means killing a man who'd kill you if he saw you first. Maybe it means killing a man in defense of your business—the way you make the money to take care of your wife and child. . . .[29]

Finally, even the "justified" murdering got to be too much. A man who was a boy at the time remembers walking back from the movies with Capone, "The Enforcer" Nitti, and "Machine Gun" McGurn, on a summer evening:

As we passed this place, this home, we stopped. . . . [T]here was a family sitting there having dinner. And [Capone] says to me, "Boy, what I wouldn't give to be able to sit with my family with the shades up like that eating dinner." He says, "Boy, don't you ever get involved in this kind of life. If you do, and I'm alive, I'll personally kill you."[30]

So Capone tried to find a home far away from Chicago. In the spring of 1928, he bought a home on Palm Island near Miami, Florida. He stayed there as often as he could. In fact, he was there when the St. Valentine's Day Massacre happened.

chapter three

LIFE IN THE DAYS OF AL CAPONE

LIFESTYLE—To prohibit something is a way of saying "no," and what Prohibition said "no" to was making, transporting, and/or selling alcoholic beverages.

Prohibition

It seemed like such a good idea at the time. There had been a Protestant religious movement to get rid of drinking since the 1800s. A drawing published in 1876 showed a "Temperance Procession." It was like a protest rally today; one of the marchers in the drawing carried a banner that said "All's Right When Daddy Comes Home Sober." A drawing published in 1846 titled "The Drunkards Progress—From the First Glass to the Grave" showed images of a young man going through the following stages:

- Step 1. A glass with a friend.

- Step 2. A glass to keep the cold out.

- Step 3. A glass too much.

- Step 4. Drunk and riotous.

- Step 5. A confirmed drunkard.

- Step 6. Poverty and disease.

- Step 7. Forsaken by friends.

- Step 8. Desperation and crime.

- Step 9. Death by suicide.

At the bottom was a drawing of the young man's wife and child—homeless, penniless, and starving. The picture made the point that not only did the young man destroy his own life by drinking, he destroyed the lives of his family, too.

Not everyone felt the same way about drinking. Another set of images published in 1879 proclaimed beer to be "A Healthy Drink," "A National Drink," "A Friendly Drink," and "A Family Drink." (This last point was illustrated by a drawing of a mother giving beer to the baby on her lap.)[1]

But during World War I, there were special pressures that lined up with the Temperance Movement. The United States entered the war in 1917 and soon there was not enough food and fuel for both the war and regular life. So the United States passed laws to control prices and to control how much people could have. (Controlling the amount people could have was called rationing. People were supposed to get only their share or "ration," and that was it.) Both sugar and grain—important ingredients for popular alcoholic beverages—were rationed.

It was during this shortage that the Anti-Saloon League claimed liquor production used up enough grain to make 11 million loaves of bread a day.[2] A temporary Prohibition was enacted during the war in order to save grain so that it could be used for food. During the war, then, Prohibition seemed both necessary and right.

But a permanent Prohibition would require an amendment to the United States Constitution. Congress cannot do that; three fourths of the states have to agree before the Constitution can be changed. So, in 1917, as the war effort was gearing up, Congress began the process of asking the states for their votes. State lawmakers voted on the proposed constitutional amendment during the war when people were living with rationing already. Then, even though the war ended in November 1918, enough states had voted in favor that Congress declared the Eighteenth Amendment passed (ratified it) on January 29, 1919. Prohibition went into effect in January 1920.

The key section of the Eighteenth Amendment (Section 1) went like this:

> After one year from the ratification of this article the manu-
> facture, sale, or transportation of intoxicating liquors within,
> the importation thereof into, or the exportation thereof from
> the United States . . . for beverage purposes is hereby
> prohibited.[3]

The constitutional amendment explains the basic idea, but it does not explain how Prohibition would work. So Congress passed the Prohibition Act (also known as the "Volstead Act" for the Minnesota congressman, Andrew Volstead, who introduced it) to provide the working details.

There was a problem, however. The choice between food and drink seemed clear enough when there were not enough

This poster was published during World War I. While some people argued that making *liquor took resources away from food*, this poster argued that buying *liquor took resources away from food*, too.

crops to go around. But after the war, the United States entered a time of plenty known as the Roaring Twenties. By the time the Eighteenth Amendment took effect, people did not want to do without alcohol anymore. A lot of people wanted to go back to drinking.

Instead of disappearing, places to buy a drink (known as speakeasies) flourished during the Prohibition. It was estimated in 1929 that there were thirty-two thousand speakeasies in New York City alone.[4] But because speakeasies were illegal, they would hide behind (or perhaps underneath) a regular, legal business. To get into the speakeasy, people would go to the special door and give the password. The classic example of a speakeasy password was "Joe sent me."

People who were in the winemaking or beer-brewing business before Prohibition figured out how to keep their businesses going during Prohibition, too. They sold products that were not alcoholic, but could be turned into wine or beer at home. Some came with detailed directions—but because the result was illegal, the directions were labeled what *not* to do. The number of acres used to grow wine grapes expanded almost seven-fold during Prohibition. [5]

Transporting alcoholic beverages was a challenge, too. Tall boots—called "Russian boots"—that had enough room to hide a flask became popular. One story says that a young man on a ship filled life preservers with booze. But when he tossed the life preservers to a friend coming to meet him in a boat, the extra-heavy preservers broke the friend's arm! Another story says that a woman who had tied six pint

This woman is hiding a flask of liquor in her boot. Perhaps this is why dealing in illegal liquor was known as "bootlegging."

bottles of booze to her girdle was caught; three of the bottles were supposedly hanging under each side of her skirt. Some people favored a garden hose—either tied around their waists for small amounts, or stretched across rooftops to move gallons.

The "Terrible Gennas," enemies of Capone's, demonstrated the dangers of illegal brewing. They started by getting a permit to handle industrial alcohol, which is poisonous. But they only shipped a small amount to industries, the rest they doctored up with colorings and flavorings to sell as fake liquor. The trouble was they were not very good at fixing it to be not poisonous. What happened to some of the people who drank it? They were in horrible pain for several days, saw things that were not there, went temporarily insane, went permanently blind, or died.

Even so, the Terrible Gennas could not produce enough bootleg booze to meet demand. So they decided to increase their supply by having people living in Chicago's Italian section brew it at home. The Gennas provided the equipment, ingredients (mash, sugar, and yeast), and instructions. They also explained how to illegally tap into waterlines and gas lines in order to get those things for free. On top of that, the Gennas paid each household fifteen dollars per day—at a time when fifteen dollars a *week* would be a good wage.

Soon there were thousands of stills—equipment for "cooking" alcohol—cooking away. One teenager who delivered butter and eggs in the neighborhood said, "You walked down Taylor Street and you could damn near get drunk on the fumes!"[6]

But things were not all good. Sometimes a still would blow up, killing the people who were watching it. And once, when police looked through one hundred barrels of mash taken from the neighborhood, they found dead rats in every single one.

Corruption

How could people get away with all this illegal activity? Where were the people in charge of law enforcement?

Amazingly enough, when Prohibition first went into effect, the people supporting it did not expect much trouble. The first Prohibition commissioner said confidently, "This law will be obeyed in cities, large and small, and in villages, and where it is not obeyed it will be enforced. . . ."[7] Indeed, finding violators was thought to be simple—the women in their lives would turn them in. (Remember the drawing showing how drinking destroyed a man's family?)

Very few Prohibition officers were hired and the pay was not very good (about two thousand dollars a year—less than garbage collectors made). On the other hand, Prohibition raised the prices of alcoholic beverages—a drink that used

THESE DECOCTIONS
KILLED
215 Chicagoans During
1923

This photo shows how poisonous some bootleg drinks could be. The people who put this display together in 1924 were trying to convince Congress that Prohibition was not a good idea.

to cost ten cents could now cost as much as a dollar. So bootleggers had plenty of money.

Here is one example of what happened. A Prohibition agent was waiting to grab a truck loaded with whiskey as it came out of a garage. He was feeling bad. Just two days before, a judge had dismissed a good case against a bootlegger that the agent had worked hard on. The bootlegger had secretly paid the judge, so he could get away with his illegal activities. And if that were not bad enough, the judge reprimanded the agent for "snooping." While the agent was sitting in his car thinking this over, a man walked up to him and said, "If you will turn your back for sixty seconds, I'll give you $10,000." The agent looked away, the truck disappeared around the corner, the man said, "Your sixty seconds are up. Thank you," and he slipped the agent ten, brand-new one-thousand-dollar bills. The agent had just earned in sixty easy seconds what it would have taken him five years to earn on his agent's salary.[8]

Another time, the head of the New York Prohibition Squad was concerned that many of his poorly paid Prohibition agents were being driven to work in limousines. He called all his agents to a meeting in a room with a large table. Once everyone was there, he told the agents to put both their hands on the table. Then he barked, "Now, every one of you [men] with a diamond ring is fired. Don't move them hands!" [9] He fired half his agents that day.

The police were not any better. The police chief in Chicago admitted that about half of *his* force was involved in bootlegging, too. They were not only involved in collecting payoffs, but also in actually selling booze. There were so many police officers going to the Terrible Gennas' warehouse for bribes that the Gennas had to get the official list from the local police station; police from other neighborhoods were slipping into line. When the United States District Attorney ordered a raid on gangsters in Chicago Heights, the *first* place the raiders seized was the local police station.

When police took bribes for ignoring Prohibition violations, it became harder to crack down on gangsters for other violations. Once, some new police recruits burst in on a

This picture, taken during Prohibition, shows a still, a home-made machine used to make alcohol illegally at home. This particular machine was captured by agents from the Bureau of Internal Revenue.

gang's headquarters and ended up capturing a lot of weapons. When they were proudly showing off the weapons at the station, the police captain angrily ordered them to "Take that stuff back!"[10]

Even if gangsters *were* miraculously put in jail, it did not make much difference. A couple of Capone's rivals, Terry Druggan and Frankie Lake, were jailed in the summer of 1924. During their sentence, a reporter went to interview them. He was greeted with, "Mr. Druggan isn't in today."

"All right," he replied, "I'll talk to the other one."

"Mr. Lake also had an appointment downtown. They'll

be back after dinner," the reporter was told.[11] Even though they were sentenced to jail, the gangsters came and went whenever they wanted to.

Gangsters also interfered with elections. In elections, people vote for the men and women they want to run the country, the states, the counties, and the towns. Gangsters, of course, wanted people who would not interfere with the gangsters' activities to be elected. But gangsters cheated. Sometimes people were murdered. Sometimes gangsters would bomb a candidate's house to scare the candidate into quitting. Sometimes a gangster would ask voters waiting in line who they were voting for, and if he did not like the answer, the gangster would grab the ballot out of the voter's hands, "fix" it, and stand there with his hand on his gun until the voter put the "correct" vote into the ballot box.

Given all the money that bootleggers were making and given their often successful efforts to influence elections, gangsters could buy off not only Prohibition agents and police, but also judges, juries, lawyers, mayors, and even governors.

The situation was so bad in Chicago that six prominent businessmen got together to try to do something about it. They were so afraid of what gangsters might do to them that they kept their names secret. Only the chairman, Robert Isham Randolph, was known. Even though their official name was "The Citizens Committee for the Prevention and Punishment of Crime," the newspapers called them the "Secret Six."

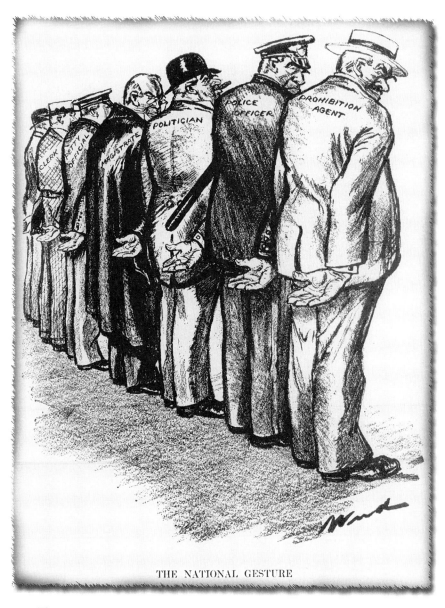

THE NATIONAL GESTURE

This cartoon, printed in 1926, shows how widespread corruption among public officials seemed to be. People from all walks of life hold out their hands looking for money.

Gangsters

Gangsters were corrupting both the legal process and the political process. They were poisoning the public with fake booze and murdering people. Still, the public admired gangsters. Crowds at racetracks and baseball games cheered Al Capone, and Capone's hotel headquarters was one of the attractions showed off by tourist buses.

The murders were overlooked because the general feeling (however untrue) was that gangsters only hurt each other. Will Rogers, a popular humorist at the time, joked in a 1928 letter he wrote to *The New York Times* that:

> You can kid about Chicago and its crooks, but they have the smartest way of handling their crooks of any city. They get the rival gangs to kill off each other and all the police have to do is just referee and count up the bodies. . . .[12]

As for violating Prohibition, Capone asked, "Who doesn't?"[13]

Movies about gangsters became very popular. In most of the gangster films of the 1920s, the gangster was a guy to look up to—he intelligently figured out ways to bring people the "light amusements" they wanted, and his lifestyle included fancy clothes, beautiful women, and powerful friends.

How did actual gangsters feel about this? Capone was against it. He said:

> You know, these gang pictures, that's terrible kid stuff. . . . They're doing nothing but harm to [kids] . . . these gang movies are making a lot of kids want to be tough guys and they don't serve any useful purpose.[14]

Federal Income Tax

A federal income tax was enacted to raise money during the Civil War. But the federal government did not need the extra money when the war was over, so the tax expired at the end of 1871. After more than twenty years without an income tax, another one was passed in 1894, about the time Capone's parents came to the United States. But this one was declared unconstitutional by the Supreme Court in April 1895.[15]

So it took a bit of work to have a federal income tax at all, then even more work to set up an arrangement that could be used to jail gangsters.

First was the matter of making the federal income tax legal. As the Supreme Court pointed out, the federal government could have an income tax. There was a federal income tax during the Civil War, and Article One, Section 8 of the Constitution said, in part: "Congress shall have Power To lay and collect Taxes. . . ."

The problem, the Supreme Court explained, was that other parts of the Constitution placed restrictions on how the income tax should be handled. The 1894 income tax was not handled right and that was why the Supreme Court said it was unconstitutional.

To fix the problem, the Constitution would have to be changed, amended. So the Sixteenth Amendment became effective in 1913. This amendment says: "The Congress shall have power to lay and collect taxes on incomes, from whatever source derived, without apportionment among the several States, and without regard to any census or enumeration."

That solved the problem of how the tax should be handled.

Congress did not waste any time acting on it, either. That October, Congress passed a law calling for a federal income tax. The 1913 income tax was declared constitutional by the Supreme Court on January 24, 1916 (exactly a week after Al's seventeenth birthday), and the United States has had a federal income tax ever since.[16]

But the story does not end there. When the 1913 income tax was passed, it only applied to *legal* income. The law said it applied to "income derived from . . . the transaction of any *lawful* business. . . .[italics added]" After the Volstead Act passed and the liquor business became illegal, courts started to rule that any income made from bootlegging was not subject to federal income tax.

So in 1921, Congress passed a law to say that the Volstead Act did not overrule the income tax laws. In the Revenue Act of 1921, Congress fixed the definition of taxable income by taking out the word *lawful* (it now covered income from *any* business, whether lawful or unlawful). And just to make sure that the point was not missed, the Revenue Act of 1921 also added a tax specifically for alcoholic beverages.

But the government's ability to tax bootleg income had yet to be tested in the courts. In 1921, a small-time South Carolina bootlegger, Manley Sullivan, was prosecuted for not paying federal income tax. And although he may have been small-time, his lawyers made some big-time arguments.

First, his lawyers argued that if individuals were engaged in illegal activities, then it was not right for the government to make money from those illegal activities. The government should not get money by taxing illegal income.

Then they argued that filing a tax return on illegal activities violated Sullivan's Fifth Amendment rights. The Fifth Amendment of the Constitution of the United States says (in part): "No person . . . shall be compelled in any criminal case to be a witness against himself. . . ."

Federal income tax forms ask for the source of a person's income. If Sullivan submitted a tax return that named a criminal source for the income, then he would be "testifying" that he was involved in a criminal activity and that "testimony" could be used against him in court. Requiring Sullivan to submit the tax return, his lawyers argued, was the same thing as requiring him to testify against himself in a criminal case. His lawyers concluded: Since the Constitution said the government could not force a person to testify against him- or herself, it was illegal for the government to require Sullivan to file a tax return on his illegal income.

They were pretty good arguments. They even won in the federal appeals court. But when the case got to the Supreme Court, the Supreme Court decided on May 16, 1927, that Sullivan *could* be held guilty of tax violations.[17]

Responding to Sullivan's first argument, the Supreme Court said, in effect, "The Revenue Act of 1921 says income from all business is taxable, it's clear that they meant illegal businesses, too, and we don't see any good reason to change it."[18]

As for Sullivan's second argument, the Supreme Court ruled that Sullivan's lawyers were taking the Fifth Amendment too far. The Fifth Amendment should not be used as an excuse to avoid paying taxes. If the tax return asked questions the taxpayer did not want to answer, the Court said, then the taxpayer should note objections on the return. The taxpayer should not avoid filing (and paying) altogether.

So Al Capone had been head of the outfit in Chicago for over two years before it was finally settled that people could be sent to jail for not filing—and not paying—income taxes on illegal income.

chapter four

THE ROAD TO COURT

CATCHING CAPONE—There were two major branches of the effort to jail Al Capone, one headed by Eliot Ness, and one headed by Elmer Irey.

Eliot Ness

Eliot Ness was the son of a baker who had come to the United States from Norway with his wife, Emma. Ness was about four years younger than Al Capone, and did not have any better luck than Capone when it came to nicknames in school. Ness's nickname was "Elegant Mess."[1] Unlike Capone, Ness did finish high school and graduated from college at the University of Chicago.

As a boy, Eliot Ness loved to read Sherlock Holmes detective stories. For years, he dreamed of becoming a detective and catching the bad guys just like Holmes. But his dream did not come true right away. The closest he could get after graduating from college was a job investigating insurance claims. His next job was not much better—he became a Prohibition agent.

His big chance came in 1929. Ness's oldest sister was married to Alexander Jamie, who had just begun to work for the Secret Six. One day, Ness and Jamie were having lunch and talking about how corrupt many law enforcement agents were. How could law-abiding citizens hope to combat crime when all the law enforcement agents were on the side of the crooks?

Jamie said something about "one bad apple in the barrel spoiling the rest," and it got Ness to thinking. Instead of having a whole barrel of apples, why not have a handful that you could keep an eye on? Why not pick apples that you know are good ones to start with? And if it works for apples, it should work for Prohibition agents. Ness excitedly explained his new idea to Jamie about having a small, carefully chosen band of agents to avoid being corrupted by payoffs. A group like that could really do something about crooks. Jamie agreed to pass the idea along.

On September 28, 1929, Ness was called in to see the District Attorney for the Chicago area, George E. Q. Johnson. Johnson reacted to Ness's idea the way Ness had hoped: "I like it! I like the whole plan!"[2] Encouraged, Ness asked Johnson if he could arrange things so Ness could be named to the squad. Johnson's prompt answer disappointed Ness. "I'm sorry, I can't do that," said Johnson.[3]

It took tremendous self-control not to yell back that it was not fair. After all, he had come up with the idea. Why couldn't he be in the group? Before Ness could think of something useful to say, Johnson continued: "I'm sorry, I can't do that because the leader of this squad is going to have a free hand—and not even I am going to tell you whom you should choose."[4]

It took a moment for Johnson's words to sink in—"not even I am going to tell *you* whom *you* should choose." It was a moment Johnson enjoyed, and he smiled when Ness's jaw dropped as Ness realized that not only was he going to be *in* the group, he was going to *lead* it. Johnson confirmed it: "That's right, Mr. Ness, you're going to get the chance to make your own plan work. And it's going to be up to you to pick your own men."[5]

And pick them he did. Their task was twofold. First, they were to collect evidence to support Prohibition charges against Capone and his men. Second, they were to close down breweries and stills—not to dry up the gang's booze, but to dry up the gang's money. Less money meant less ability to buy off justice.

It was not hard to find breweries. Their aroma was so strong that if the wind was right, a brewery could be smelled from half a mile away. Winter brought its own way of finding breweries. While most buildings had white icicles or clear icicles, breweries had yellow icicles (from the beer produced).

But it took a little practice to get the hang of capturing a brewery. Capone's breweries had escape routes out the back. They also had steel doors inside of the wooden ones. The first time Ness tried to hack through a brewery door with an axe, it made such a racket and took so long that when they finally got in, the brewery was empty of gangsters.

Ness came up with the idea of a ramming truck—a ten-ton flatbed truck with special bumpers and handles on the inside for his men to hang onto as the truck rammed through both sets of doors. He also came up with the idea of finding the exits and assigning men to guard them. They captured a lot of breweries that way, and captured quite a few trucks along with them.

Payoffs had worked on Prohibition agents before, so it was not surprising that the gangsters would try to buy off Ness and his men. An informant offered Ness an envelope with two thousand dollars, along with an offer of two thousand dollars each week if he would order his men to back off. Ness refused.

The same day, the gangsters also tried to bribe a couple of Ness's men. To make sure the men couldn't refuse the money, the mobsters waited until the two men were out driving, then the mobsters drove up beside them and tossed a big roll of bills through their open car window. But Ness's men were determined to show they were not going to accept bribes. They took off after the mob car, caught up with it, and threw the money back in the mobsters' open window—hitting the driver in the eye and nearly causing an accident. Ness's men had made their point.

Afterward, when Ness's whole group was together and they were telling each other what happened, one of the men jokingly said, "You can tell the world!" And that got Ness to thinking. Why not? He called reporters to set up a press

This picture, taken in 1922, shows a dog trained to use its keen sense of smell to find a bottle of illegal liquor. Eliot Ness used his nose to find entire breweries.

conference to "tell the world" that Eliot Ness and his men could not be bought.

One newspaper article after the press conference started with "Eliot Ness and his young agents have proved to Al Capone that they are untouchable." Another newspaper picked up the words and put "The Untouchables" over a newsphoto of the group. The name caught on, and they were known as "The Untouchables" after that.[6]

But it was not all glory and popping flashbulbs for Ness and his men. As Ness wrote later: "It isn't the facing danger that cuts you up inside. It's the waiting and the not knowing what's coming."[7]

The gangsters knew that, too; they not only played war games, they played mind games. They planted false information about Ness. They let Ness find out that they were following him. They also started calling Ness each day, the same voice with the same message: "Hello, big shot. How does it feel to be waiting to get it? It won't be long now."[8] Then the caller would hang up.

When ignoring the phone calls for almost a week did not work, Ness interrupted with, "What's the matter with you punks? Can't you find any old ladies to rob or any kids to scare?" The caller started spitting out a long string of swear words, but Ness hung up. The next call Ness interrupted with, "You grave robbers haven't got the guts to shoot anybody who's looking" and then Ness hung up right away. They did not try calling again.[9]

Ness found an even more public way to fight the mind games. Right in the middle of their war on bootleggers, Ness and his men had to move the captured trucks from one town garage to another. Ness decided to make a parade of it, a real show of force. He ordered the trucks—all forty-five of them—be polished. Then he planned a route that took them right in front of the hotel where Capone had his main office. Just to make sure Capone did not miss it, Ness called him: "Well, Snorky, I just wanted to tell you that if you look out your front windows . . . at exactly eleven o'clock you'll see something that should interest you."[10]

Ness heard later that Capone got so angry watching the parade that "he carried on like a ravin' maniac" and "they had a [hard] time calming him down."[11]

Ness thought of the parade and the press conferences as moves in the war of nerves with the gangsters. But they had another effect, too. The public had seemed to believe that gangsters were unstoppable.[12] The public needed to hear there were law enforcement officials who could not be bought and that something really could be done. When Ness started his job, the public was calling the mob with tips on The Untouchables' location and plans. As the news stories of The Untouchables' exploits continued, the public starting calling Ness with tips on the mob's locations and plans. The tide was beginning to turn.

Elmer Irey

Elmer Lincoln Irey was the first head of the federal Treasury Department's Special Intelligence Unit or "SIU." Eleven years older than Al Capone, he was born in 1888 in Kansas City and raised in Washington, D.C. Irey started his working life as a kind of secretary in the post office, then worked his way up to Postal Inspector, earning eighteen hundred dollars a year.

Irey got his big break in 1919 when an old friend remembered him. He and Joseph Callan used to be clerks together. But then Callan had moved on, becoming a special assistant to the Commissioner of Internal Revenue. When the commissioner told Callan he wanted to set up a special unit, Callan said, "Maybe we can get some Post Office Inspectors. They can spot a missing penny quicker than anybody in the world."[13] Callan sent for Irey and the SIU was born.

Many people think that because Capone obviously had a

lot of money, yet never filed a federal income tax return that the case was closed. But it was not that easy.

The Supreme Court decision against Manley Sullivan paved the way to jail people for income tax violations on illegal income, and there were at least two ways to do it. There was a misdemeanor, a minor charge, for failing to file a return, and there was the felony, a serious charge, for tax evasion.

The "failure to file" law said:

> Any person required under this title to pay any tax . . . who willfully fails . . . to make such return . . . at the time or times required by law or regulations, shall, . . . be guilty of a misdemeanor and, upon conviction thereof, be fined not more than $10,000, or imprisoned for not more than one year, or both, together with the costs of prosecution.[14]

"Together with the costs of prosecution" means that someone who has been convicted has to pay the government back for all the money the government spent on the court case.

Proving that someone did not file a tax return is not enough. For someone to be convicted of failure to file, the government also has to prove a) that they owed a tax *and* b) the person did not file the return *on purpose* knowing that they owed a tax. Not filing because you were too sick, for example, is not a crime.

The tax evasion law said:

> any person who willfully attempts in any manner to evade or defeat any tax imposed by this title or the payment thereof, shall . . . be guilty of a felony and, upon conviction thereof, be fined not more than $10,000, or imprisoned for not

more than five years, or both, together with the costs of prosecution.[15]

The felony count goes one step further. In order to prove people guilty of tax evasion, the government has to prove:

- that they owe a tax (This includes proving that they have taxable income. They would not be guilty of income tax violations if the money came from sources that are not subject to tax. Money made gambling is income.);

- that they did not pay the tax *on purpo*se knowing that they owed the tax; and

- they took some additional steps to evade paying the tax (in addition to simply not paying or not filing).

Notice that "willfulness" is included in both laws. The government has to prove that someone did not meet his or her income tax obligations on purpose (not, for example, because that person really believed the income was not taxable). A corrupt politician who was prosecuted about this time made an interesting legal argument. His argument basically was: "If you want to know what I was thinking, why ask the jury? They weren't there. The only person who could possibly know what I was thinking is *me*. I'm telling you that I honestly thought my income was not taxable—and that should be the end of it."[16]

Sounds logical, except for one thing. If courts are required to believe whatever defendants said they were thinking, defendants might lie and nobody would be convicted. So the appeals court ruled that it was acceptable to let the jury decide.[17]

Finally, it is important to know that tax "avoidance" is not tax "evasion." Tax avoidance is taking *legal* steps to reduce the amount of taxes owed. In tax avoidance, a taxpayer is playing by the rules and has learned how to use the rules to his or her advantage. That is fine.

Tax evasion, on the other hand, is *not* playing by the rules. Tax evasion occurs when someone deliberately cheats—by lying, or hiding money, for instance. That is not acceptable.

Back to Irey and his SIU. They were also aiming for other higher-ups in Capone's organization as practice for getting Capone: Capone's brother Ralph, Jake "Greasy Thumb" Guzik, and Frank "The Enforcer" Nitti.

They got a clue about Ralph, first. It seems that the Chicago office of the Bureau of Internal Revenue (now the Internal Revenue Service or IRS) had a very pushy agent named Eddie Waters. He used to go into gambling houses and bother gangsters about paying their income taxes. In 1926, he finally got through to Ralph Capone. When Capone complained that it was such a hassle filling out the tax forms, Waters made him an offer: "Bottles, you just tell me what you made and I'll fill it out for you. Then all you gotta do is sign."[18]

So, Capone told Waters how much he made. (Of course, he gave income amounts that were much too small.) Waters filled out the forms. (They showed Ralph Capone owed a little over four thousand dollars—pocket change for him.)

Waters brought the forms back to Ralph Capone and Capone signed them. *Then he never got around to paying.*

After waiting a while to give Ralph Capone time to pay, the government started the legal process to take away some of Capone's assets. So Ralph Capone and his lawyer gave the IRS a letter in October 1927 saying he was flat broke. He could, however, borrow one thousand dollars to give to the IRS, if the IRS would forget the rest of what he owed.

Well, the SIU knew Ralph had more money than that, so it went to work trying to prove it. The agent assigned to finding Ralph Capone's "hidden" income went to his boss after several weeks and said:

> Chief, . . . you know Bottles has ten grand [thousand dollars] in his pocket. . . . Everybody in Chicago knows it. Please, Chief, can I go down and stick this gun in his belly and take the dough away from him? I'll do it right in the middle of the street. We'll have a thousand witnesses. Please, Chief.[19]

But the government was not going to do it that way. It went back to digging—and talking to the owner of a gambling house whose financial records had been seized in a raid. In order to stay out of jail himself, the owner dropped enough hints that Nels Tessem, one of Irey's men, was able to piece together (from bank deposit slips, cancelled checks, and bank records) that Ralph Capone had been keeping his money in a series of bank accounts under false names. They were able to document that since 1924, those accounts had seen over $1.5 million dollars—and on the day Ralph Capone swore in writing that he was broke, his account held over $25,000.[20]

The government had what it needed. Ralph Capone was indicted, formally charged, with tax evasion on October 29, 1929. "Indicted" did not mean he was proven guilty yet; "indicted" means that a grand jury had decided there was enough evidence against him that it was worth having a trial. There was no point in putting everyone through a criminal trial if the government's case did not seem strong enough to win in court.

The SIU was finally able to track down what it needed against The Enforcer because it ran across a check—one check—that Nitti had signed on the back, taking some of the income from a gambling operation. Tessem took the one-thousand-dollar check to the bank where it had been cashed and looked through all the deposit slips and transaction records for the day, but nothing had Nitti's name on it. Using the bank's deposit slips and receipts, Tessem built his own ledger for the bank for that day. (This is like putting together a puzzle with thousands of pieces, only doing it with lots and lots of "adding up.")

Tessem's financial records showed that the bank's records were exactly one thousand dollars off—and the bank president admitted he had a deal with Nitti to cash Nitti's checks without showing them in the bank's records. The bank president agreed to show Tessem the books that had *all* of Nitti's official transactions on them. Nitti was indicted for three years' worth of tax evasion in March 1930.

Guzik had also signed checks on the back like Nitti, and like Ralph had marched money through accounts with fake names. But the SIU was able to come up with a key additional piece—a witness. A former teller at one of the banks told Irey's men that a man named Fred deposited the money for Guzik. He remembered Fred, the teller explained, because one day when they were going through their usual transactions, a cockroach appeared and Fred turned as white as if he had seen a ghost. Fred was so shaken up, he forgot to give the teller his usual five dollar tip—something the teller *did not* forget.

Fred, who turned out to be Fred Ries, a cashier at Capone's premier gambling establishment—almost got away. Frank Wilson, one of the lead SIU men on the case, did not know where Ries was until Wilson found a St. Louis gangster on his way to St. Paul; the gangster told Wilson that Ries was in St. Louis.

Wilson and Tessem went immediately to St. Louis and headed for the post office. Fortunately, Ries was using his own name. When Wilson and Tessem asked, people working at the post office could say they were about to deliver a special delivery letter to Ries. Wilson and Tessem followed the mail carrier. They found Ries reading a letter from Greasy Thumb's brother-in-law, telling Ries to go to California right away and giving him the money to do it!

Although they had found Ries just in time, he refused to talk. Then Wilson and Tessem remembered the cockroach.

Wilson made arrangements for Ries to be put in a small-town jail that was crawling with insects. After four days, a desperate Ries said to Wilson: "The bedbugs are eating me alive! I'll explain those cashier's checks. But for God's sake get me away from these bugs!!"[21]

Ries testified before a grand jury and Guzik was indicted in October 1930.

The next problem was keeping Ries from being killed. As Irey explained later: "He had a great deal of information we needed, and if we jailed him we would have a hostile witness; if we freed him we would have a dead one. So he traveled."[22]

Because the government did not have any money to protect witnesses, the Secret Six paid over ten thousand dollars of their own money. Ries, accompanied by a federal agent, hit the road. He even spent some time in South America.

But Al Capone was a lot tougher. As Wilson explained to Irey, "Nitti and Guzik got careless. Al hasn't."[23] Irey's men spent countless hours working, but were no closer to getting Al Capone than when they started. For months, Wilson worked eighteen-hour days in a small, windowless room in the old post office building, looking through document after document. (Working an eighteen-hour day is like starting work at 6:00 A.M., working straight through until midnight, then going to bed and starting all over again the next day at 6:00 A.M.)

After midnight one summer night in 1930, a bleary-eyed, exhausted Wilson started packing up to go home. He accidentally locked the filing cabinet where documents were supposed to go, so he poked around looking for another place to put them. He found a place, but inside was a dusty old package wrapped in brown paper and tied with string. He opened the package and started idly poking through the records inside—and found what he had been seeking for over two years. The entries showed income from a large-scale gambling operation for 1924 through 1926 and that one-sixth of the income went to "Al." That *had* to be Al Capone.

But they had to prove it. The records were kept by hand, so Irey's men looked through countless slips of paper trying to match the handwriting. They finally figured out that one of the bookkeepers was Leslie Adelbert Shumway (people usually called him "Lou"). But Lou was missing. It was not until February 1931 that they got a tip—Shumway was working at a Florida dog track.

Wilson headed to Florida, and after a little hunting around, found Shumway at the Biscayne Bay Kennel Club. Shumway, like Ries before him, denied everything.

Wilson got tough. If Shumway would not help, Wilson said, he would send a deputy sheriff to the dog track to announce loudly that he was looking for Leslie Shumway to be a witness against Al Capone.

Frank Wilson is the man who found the critical gambling house ledgers. He also convinced the two key witnesses to talk. This picture was taken the year after Al Capone's tax trial.

Wilson asked Shumway to estimate how long he would remain alive after a scene like that. But there was an alternative, Wilson told him: "Play ball, Lou, and I'll guarantee that Mrs. Shumway will not become a widow."[24] Shumway decided to talk.

But he had to talk fast. It was now the end of February 1931, and the evidence they had on Capone in those records went back to 1924. If they did not get an indictment against Capone by March 15, they would not be able to bring tax evasion charges for 1924. (This was a "statute of limitations" issue. At the time, tax evasion charges had to be brought within six years after the filing date or they could never be brought to court. Since March 15, 1925, had been the deadline for filing a 1924 tax return, they did not have much time.) Wilson got Shumway back to Chicago and in front of a secret grand jury as soon as he could. The grand jury indicted Capone for 1924 tax evasion on March 13, 1931—two days before the deadline.

Capone, meanwhile, was not sitting around doing nothing. He had hired Lawrence P. Mattingly, a famous tax lawyer from Washington, D.C.

As a tax expert, Mattingly would have known about the Bureau of Internal Revenue policy that taxpayers who offered to pay before they were sued were not prosecuted. In fact, it was a policy that had been established by Irey himself. So back on March 23, 1930, Mattingly started negotiations to settle Capone's tax obligations with a letter to a federal Internal Revenue agent in Chicago:

Dear Sir:

Mr. Alphonse Capone . . . has authorized me to make an exact computation of income tax liability for the year 1929 and prior years, the amount of which he will pay as soon as determined. Mr. Capone has never filed income tax returns.[25]

Mattingly had several meetings in Chicago with the Bureau of Internal Revenue. Then the bureau asked Mattingly to put Capone's offer to settle in writing. So he did. In a letter dated September 20, 1930, Mattingly started with legal language that said the letter was only part of the settlement talks and they should not use the letter against Capone in court. He used legal language that said he was not swearing that the information in the letter was actual fact, but it was true as far as he knew. In the middle, he explained that Al Capone's share of the illegal business was one-sixth.

But it was only a *policy* not to prosecute taxpayers who offered to settle. It was not the law. On June 5, 1931, a grand jury indicted Capone for tax evasion for the years 1925, 1926, 1927, 1928 and 1929. Capone was indicted for the misdemeanor "failure to file" for 1928 and 1929. (The time limit for bringing misdemeanor charges was only three years.) There were twenty-three counts altogether, including the one brought earlier for tax evasion in 1924.

A week later, based on information provided by Eliot Ness and his Untouchables, a grand jury brought *five thousand* Prohibition charges against Capone along with sixty-eight other charges.

chapter five

THE COURT

COURTROOM—Ralph Capone was the first to go to court. His tax evasion case went to trial in April 1930. It took the jury fifteen days to hear the stacks of evidence the SIU had gathered, but it only took them two and a half hours to find Ralph Capone guilty. The judge sentenced Ralph to three years in jail and ten thousand dollars in fines.

The court was even harder on Jake Guzik. After the jury found him guilty, the judge sentenced him to five years in jail and he had to pay seventeen thousand five hundred dollars in fines.

Frank Nitti, meanwhile, pleaded guilty instead of going through a trial. He was sentenced to eighteen months in prison and a ten-thousand-dollar fine.

There seemed to be a lesson here. It might be better to admit to guilt than to have the prosecutor try to prove it in court. So when Al Capone was indicted, his lawyers (now his trial lawyers, Michael Ahern and Albert Fink) contacted United States District

Attorney George E. Q. Johnson to discuss a deal—Capone would plead guilty in return for a smaller sentence (the legal term for this is "plea bargain").

Johnson was in favor of it. It is hard to predict what will happen when a case goes before a jury. Lawyers may think they have a great case, but the jury may think otherwise—and the defendant (in this case, Al Capone) could walk out of court a free man. And what if the witnesses became too afraid to talk when they had to face Capone in court? Johnson checked with his superiors (including the secretary of the treasury and the attorney general of the United States) and they gave their OK to accept a guilty plea in return for a jail sentence of two and a half years and a fine.

On June 16, 1931, Al Capone went into court. It took less than five minutes. The clerk read the three indictment numbers: one for the 1924 tax evasion, one for the tax charges for the rest of the years, and one for all those Prohibition counts. Capone softly said, "Guilty."

Judge James H. Wilkerson said he would give Capone his sentence in two weeks, but Capone's lawyers got the sentencing pushed back to July 30. That may have been their biggest mistake. It gave the newspapers plenty of time to run articles guessing what Capone's sentence would be (and some got it right, too) and then to run articles saying it was not good enough. One publication said: "Let's hear no more about Capone's defeat. The defeat is Chicago's."[1]

The delay was long enough for Al Capone to confirm the sentence and to brag about it—before the judge had even given it to him. That made the judge seem like a puppet, and

This is Judge James Wilkerson in his office. The picture was taken in 1925, about six years before Al Capone's tax trial.

that made the judge angry.[2] When everybody came back to court to hear Capone's two-and-a-half-year sentence, Judge Wilkerson had a surprise for them. He announced that he did *not* have to give the sentence everyone was expecting. Then the judge went off to hear another case and let them worry for a while.

At 2:00 P.M., they got back together and *all* the lawyers were upset, both Capone's lawyers and U.S. Attorney Johnson. (Johnson's hands shook and his voice was higher than usual).[3] They may have been thinking about what might happen to them if Capone concluded he had been double-crossed. Both sides tried to convince the judge to go along with the trade of a short sentence for the guilty pleas. But Judge Wilkerson was still angry: The deal was off. Capone's lawyers changed his pleas to "not guilty" and Judge Wilkerson scheduled Capone's trial for October. (Although Capone withdrew his "guilty" plea to the Prohibition indictment, too, the Prohibition charges were never brought up for trial. The trial was just on the income tax charges.)

Capone did not rely entirely on his lawyers. He also tried some classic mobster tactics for handling legal difficulties.

First he tried intimidation and mentioned the possibility of murder. Informants told the SIU that Capone had hired five out-of-towners to kill several top men on the tax case, including Irey and Wilson. Then word came that Capone's advisers convinced him that he would be in worse trouble if he had them murdered, so the assassins went home.

Then Capone tried bribery. He offered Irey $1.5 *million*— in cash—if the trial did not result in a jail term. Just like Ness, Irey refused.[4]

Finally, Capone's men got to work on the members of the jury. In the week before the trial, SIU's informants tipped them off that the outfit had gotten the list of men in the jury pool—even before the judge got it. Capone's mobsters were busy trying to convince all the men on the list to tell the judge that Capone was innocent, using free tickets, money, and threats. This was just what United States Attorney Johnson had been afraid of.

So Irey, Wilson, and Johnson went to see Judge Wilkerson. Irey was "almost frantic" with worry.[5] But the Judge was calm, saying: "Bring your case into court as planned, gentlemen. Leave the rest to me."[6]

On Tuesday, October 6, when the two sides got together at the courthouse, Judge Wilkerson announced that he was switching jury pools with another judge. The men the mob had worked on trooped down the hall and a new bunch filed in.

As soon as the new jury members found out what case

The man who is tied up is Uncle Sam; he represents the government. This cartoon shows how people thought the government was helpless to do anything about Al Capone.

they were to hear, fifty out of the sixty asked to be excused. But the judge only excused eighteen, and the lawyers were able to agree on a jury of twelve. The jury members were kept together and watched over day and night during the trial.

When the trial began on October 7, the government started first. It had to tell the court what it thought the defendant was guilty of and why. Without that information, there would be nothing for the defendant to argue against.

The government's lawyers (usually Johnson's assistants, although Johnson was there) argued Capone was guilty of tax evasion and failure to file. They presented a witness to testify that Capone had never filed income tax returns, not under "Al Capone" or under a false name.

They then had to prove Capone had income. They started by calling as witnesses the men who had raided the Hawthorne Smoke Shop on May 16, 1925—the Reverend Henry Hoover, Charles Bragg, and David Morgan. These men testified that Capone said he owned the place, and acted like he owned it. The government strengthened the ownership point by having Shumway and Ries testify that Capone acted like an owner. They also had Shumway testify that when he was cashier (a period of time that overlapped 1924, 1925, and 1926), the gambling joint had taken in over half a million dollars.

This testimony argued that Capone had income he was supposed to pay income tax on, and that he had not done so. To convict him on either the misdemeanor or the felony, the government had to show that Capone knew he had to pay the taxes and he did not pay them on purpose.

This is one of the courtrooms in the building where Al Capone's tax trial was held. This picture, taken facing the judge's bench, was taken in 1964.

To show knowledge and intent, the government did something controversial. It used the letter that Capone's tax attorney, Lawrence Mattingly, had written with Capone's offer to settle. Capone's defense attorneys argued vigorously that the letter should not be allowed as evidence. (Offers to settle are generally not used as evidence in court.) But Judge Wilkerson let the prosecution use the letter.

This was a big win for the government, because the letter helped to show that Capone knew he had to pay taxes. It also confirmed that he had taxable income, and that he owed taxes that he had not paid.

Capone seemed not to realize the importance of the government's move. When he was back in his headquarters that night, he had a tailor come to measure him for new suits. "You don't need to be ordering fancy duds," said Frankie Rio, who had been right about attacks on Capone before. "You're going to prison. Why don't you have a suit made with stripes on it?"[7]

But Capone was unshakable: "I'm going to Florida for a nice, long rest, and I need some new clothes before I go."[8]

Then the government did something very interesting. Over several days, in front of a jury of "small-town trades-men, mechanics and farmers" (only one was from Chicago) they paraded lots of witnesses who talked about how much money Capone spent. They talked about the thousands and thousands of dollars Al Capone had spent on parties and clothes and furniture and landscaping and telephone bills—amounts of money that seem amazing even now.

Why would the government do this? The mere fact that Capone was spending a lot of money did not necessarily mean that the money was taxable. For example, if class-mates are spending a lot of money, that does not mean they have well-paying jobs; often it means they have rich rela-tives. Gifts received from rich relatives are not subject to income tax. Capone's lawyers quite properly objected. But Judge Wilkerson replied, "I presume that what he paid out he must have taken in" and the testimony continued.[9]

One of the last witnesses was Ries, who described how money was handled using false names—evidence that somebody was trying to cheat. (Whether the cheating showed intent to evade taxes was for the jury to decide. For example, when Ralph Capone was asked about the false names on his bank accounts, he said it had nothing to do with trying to cheat on his income taxes. He said he did it because he was running an illegal business.)

At 2:20 P.M. on Tuesday, October 13, Johnson announced that the government was finished presenting its case. Now it was time for Capone's lawyers to present their side. But they were not ready. "There was no work done on this case . . . until the plea of guilty was withdrawn," protested Fink.[10] He asked for time to prepare. The judge gave Capone's lawyers until 10:00 the next morning.

Starting Wednesday, the defense lawyers tried to argue that most of what Capone made from gambling, he had lost by gambling, so he did not have enough left to tax. They tried to prove Capone's gambling losses by calling witnesses to testify about the thousands and thousands of dollars he had lost. But that meant the witnesses were also testifying about the thousands and thousands of dollars Capone had bet. Chances are, this testimony made it seem to the jury like Capone had even *more* money than the government said he had.

Finally, on Friday, October 16, the defense lawyers made their closing arguments. They argued that while the government had shown Capone spent a lot of money, it had not made a good enough case that Capone had taxable income. They argued that Capone could not have known back in 1924, 1925, and 1926 that his income was taxable. After all, the Supreme Court had not decided that illegal

This picture of Al Capone and his two lawyers was taken in court during Capone's tax trial. Capone is in the middle. Michael Ahern is on the left and Albert Fink is on the right.

income was taxable until 1927. Further, when it became clear that his income was taxable, Capone had hired a good tax attorney and tried to settle his tax obligations. Was he the kind of person who would try to duck paying something he owed? Certainly, not. As Fink pointed out, nobody ever accused Capone of not paying what he owed. Finally, Fink argued: "Do not be swayed by the argument that the defendant is a bad man. . . . Do not for that reason find him guilty of something of which he has not been proven guilty."[11]

Attorney George E. Q. Johnson made the government's final argument on Saturday, October 17. Capone did not file income tax forms and did not pay income taxes. Was the money he was spending taxable income? Or did it come from some non-taxable source like gifts? Johnson asked the jurors, in effect, "What do you think?"

He did not mention that Al Capone was the first person to open a soup kitchen in Chicago to feed people who had lost their jobs after the stock market crashed; his soup kitchen provided thousands of free meals. But whether Capone was good or bad was not what the jury was supposed to decide; the jury was supposed to decide whether Al Capone had committed tax crimes.

After giving instructions to the jury, the judge sent them out to make their decision a little after 2:30 P.M. Most of the jury decided he was guilty. But there was one person who thought he was not guilty. That juror was convinced that the letter from Capone's attorney proved that Capone was trying to pay his taxes.

It took all afternoon and into the night for the jurors to come up with a verdict on which they could all agree. The judge, the lawyers, and Al Capone were called back into court around 11:00 P.M. to hear the verdict.

chapter six

THE DECISION

THE VERDICT—Judge Wilkerson asked the jury, "Have you arrived at a verdict?" The foreperson of the jury answered, "We have, Your Honor," and the clerk of the court read the verdict out loud. Here is what the jury decided:

- On indictment number 22852 we find the defendant not guilty.

- On indictment number 23232 we find the defendant guilty on counts 1, 5, 9, 13 and 18.

- We find the defendant not guilty on counts 2, 3, 4, 6, 7, 8, 10, 11, 12, 14, 15, 16, 17, 19, 20, 21 and 22.[1]

The government lawyers left the courtroom to talk about and analyze the results.

When all was said and done, the jury had found Capone guilty for three years of tax evasion and not guilty for three years. Capone was never charged with failure to file taxes for 1924 through 1927 because the statute of limitations had passed for those years. He was found guilty of failure to file in 1928 and 1929.

Year	Failure to File (up to 1 year in prison)	Tax Evasion (up to 5 years in prison)
1924	(not charged because of statute of limitations)	Not Guilty
1925	(not charged because of statute of limitations)	Guilty
1926	(not charged because of statute of limitations)	Guilty
1927	(not charged because of statute of limitations)	Guilty
1928	Guilty	Not Guilty
1929	Guilty	Not Guilty

When the government lawyers filed back into the court-room, the government accepted the verdict.

The next issue was how much prison time to give Capone. Judge Wilkerson announced that he needed a week to think it over, and gave permission for Capone to stay out of jail in the meantime.

Everyone was back in court on Saturday, October 24, 1931, to hear what Judge Wilkerson had decided. Capone stood to hear what his fate would be.

The Judge sentenced Capone to the maximum on each count, then ruled that some of the years would be doubled up. (For example, the same five years in prison would count as the prison time for both 1925 and 1926.) All together, the sentence added up to eleven years in prison—ten of them to be spent in a federal penitentiary and the last year to be spent in the local county jail. Capone was also sentenced to pay

These are the men who decided whether Al Capone was guilty. Nobody knows which one is the man who tried to convince everyone else that Capone was innocent.

fifty thousand dollars in fines and to pay the government the cost of taking him to court.

Capone's lawyers asked if Capone could stay free while they appealed the decision. Judge Wilkerson said no. Then the judge asked a nearby United States marshal how soon he could take Capone to Leavenworth, the federal prison in Kansas. "At six-fifteen tonight, Your Honor," came the answer.[2] Capone's lawyers argued it out with the judge, and Capone went instead to the Cook County Jail.

chapter seven

THE AFTERMATH

LASTING EFFECTS—While Al Capone got settled in at the Cook County Jail, his lawyers appealed his conviction to the Federal Appeals Court for the Seventh Circuit. (The federal district courts are grouped into circuits. To appeal a district court decision, Capone's lawyers had to appeal to the appeals court for that circuit.)

Capone's lawyers argued that Capone should go free immediately, because the government was not specific enough when it charged Capone. By not saying exactly how the government thought he was guilty, it was being unfair to Capone. It had not allowed him to prepare a better defense. The verdict was also unfair, the lawyers said, because if the government was too vague, it might try suing Capone again for the same thing.

Article Six of the United States Constitution says, in part, that "In all criminal prosecutions, the accused shall enjoy the right . . . to be informed of the nature and cause of the accusation. . . ."

Article Five of the Constitution says, in part, "Nor shall any person be subject for the same offense to be twice put in jeopardy of life or limb. . . ." And there were a bunch of cases where convicted people went free because the government's indictment was too vague.

After hearing the arguments for both sides, the Appeals Court decided:

- Capone's case was different enough from the others so that he did not have to win like they did;

- Capone could have asked for more details as far back as when the indictments first came out—but did not do so;

- Capone could have objected during the trial because the lack of detail made the job of defense too hard—but did not do so;

- It was not likely that Capone could be sued for the same thing all over again.[1]

On February 27, 1932, a warden interrupted Capone while he was playing cards to tell him that the Appeals Court had decided he would remain in jail.

Capone's lawyers appealed to the Supreme Court. But, there are so many cases appealed to the Supreme Court that the Court takes only a small percentage of those cases— those that deal with an important issue in constitutional law. On May 2, 1932, the Supreme Court said it would not hear Capone's case.[2]

Meanwhile, remember how back in Chapter 3 we learned that two gangsters, Druggan and Lake, had amazing privileges in jail? There were concerns about Capone, too. After all, what good does it do to put a gangster in jail if he can continue to do whatever he wants? The following anonymous telegram was sent to both Judge Wilkerson and United States Attorney Johnson:

> WISH TO INFORM YOU THAT AL CAPONE IS USING THE COUNTY JAIL FOR HIS LIQUOR BUSINESS AND TRANSACTS FROM THERE POSSIBLY AS MUCH IF NOT MORE THAN HE USED TO AT HIS OLD HEAD-QUARTERS. . . . HIS VISITORS SEEM TO BE COMING ALL DAY LONG AS WELL AS IN THE EVENING. . . . PLEASE INVESTIGATE.[3]

Judge Wilkerson asked the FBI to investigate and Johnson did his own investigating. Johnson's investigation suggested that the only people visiting Capone were his family and his lawyers (and his mother would send him food from home). But, on December 22, 1931, as head of the Cook County Jail, Warden David T. Moneypenny, was driving back to Chicago, the car he was driving broke down—and the car turned out to be a sixteen-cylinder Cadillac that belonged to the Capones. When asked about it, Moneypenny claimed he had no idea who owned the expensive car he found himself driving.[4] Clearly, the warden was getting favors from Capone, so Capone may have been getting special treatment from the warden.

When the Supreme Court decided not to hear Capone's case, the authorities wasted no time getting him out of the local jail. The very next day they put him on the train headed for the federal penitentiary. They were not sending Al

Capone to Leavenworth. Ralph Capone, Nitti, and Guzik had been sent to Leavenworth. It was felt that the gang should be spread out more. Al Capone was sent to the federal penitentiary in Atlanta, Georgia, one of the toughest federal prisons.

Eliot Ness and his men were chosen to escort Capone from the jail to the train. The trip took Capone right past the garage where the St. Valentine's Day Massacre occurred and right past the federal building where he had lost his freedom.

When they got to Dearborn Station, Ness and his men had to muscle their way through a crowd of news reporters, photographers, and curious people so that Capone could get on the train. It was when Ness was leaving him on the train that Capone caught Ness's eye and said:

> Well, I'm on my way to do eleven years. I've got to do it, that's all. I'm not sore at anybody. Some people are lucky. I wasn't. There was too much overhead in my business anyhow, paying off all the time and replacing trucks and breweries. They ought to make it legitimate.[5]

Ness brushed aside Capone's attempt to make peace. Ness slowly shook his head and replied, "That's a strange idea coming from you. If it was legitimate, you certainly wouldn't want anything to do with it."[6]

Capone did not say anything else, but he watched Ness as he backed out of the train compartment. The two never met again.

But, something very exciting had happened while Capone's case was still pending at the Supreme Court (before the Court had officially declined to hear the case).

On April 11, 1932, the Supreme Court decided that only the three-year statute of limitations applied to tax evasion cases.[7] All of Capone's felony convictions were beyond the three-year limit—so if they were overturned, Capone would only have to spend two and a half years behind bars instead of eleven years.

Lawyers from Washington, D. C., were hired to take advantage of the three-year rule. They filed a writ of *habeas corpus* in the District Court that covered the Atlanta penitentiary. A writ of *habeas corpus* is the legal term for a lawsuit claiming a person has been wrongly imprisoned. It does not try to determine a person's innocence or guilt—the original trial and any appeals are supposed to handle that—but it does consider whether the correct legal process was followed to take away the prisoner's freedom.

The new lawyers argued that the process was wrong. Because the three-year limit applied, Capone should not have been tried for tax evasion for 1925, 1926, and 1927, and therefore should not be in jail.

This was a tough one for Judge E. Marvin Underwood. It had taken so much effort to put Capone in prison. Did Judge Underwood want to be known as the man who let Capone out? Probably not. So the judge must have been delighted when he read on in the time-limit law and found a sentence that said:

> The time during which the person committing the offense is absent from the district wherein the same is committed shall not be taken as any part of the time limited by law for the commencement of such proceedings.[8]

Capone had spent time both at his home in Miami and about ten months in Pennsylvania before the indictments were brought. The law said that time spent outside the district would not count. Suppose Capone had spent a total of three years outside of the district. The charges went back six years. Six years minus three years outside the district is three years. So the whole thing still might come under the three-year limit.

But how much time had Capone spent outside the Chicago area? That was a question about the facts. And *habeas corpus* lawsuits do not find facts; that happens at the trial.

On January 25, 1933, Judge Underwood dismissed Capone's lawsuit. (This decision was appealed all the way up to the Supreme Court, too, but it did not help.)[9]

Later this same year, Prohibition was finally overturned. In February 1933, Congress asked the states to vote on the Twenty-First Amendment that said in Section 1: "The eighteenth article of amendment of the Constitution of the United States is hereby repealed." By December 5, 1933, enough states had voted for it that it was declared a part of the Constitution and Prohibition was over. Even if Capone had gotten out of jail, the biggest part of his illegal businesses had gone away.

Capone had another plan to get out of jail as soon as he could: he would get his sentence reduced for good behavior. As he explained to reporters on the train to Atlanta: "I'll take what they give me for two reasons. One is, the only way you can expect to get a pardon is to go along and be a good prisoner. The other is, I won't have any say about it."[10]

One prison official reported of Capone, "He is a model prisoner, and obeys every order the second it is given."[11] But there were people with other plans. United States Attorney General Homer S. Cummings had a plan for a "super-prison" to hold "criminals of the vicious and irredeemable type so that their evil influence" would not affect prisoners who wanted to straighten themselves out.[12] He made arrangements to fix up an old military prison on an island in San Francisco Bay. The Spanish explorers named the island for the pelicans that used to sit on it—*Isla de los Alcatraces*—so the government called the prison that sat on it "Alcatraz." Criminals all over the country called it "The Rock," for the island made of rock on which it sat.

Because it was such a fearsome place, judges did not send people to Alcatraz. Only convicts already in federal prison could be sent there if their warden and the head of the federal Bureau of Prisons decided they were too hard to handle. For a time it was thought that violence in federal prisons went down because convicts did not want to be shipped to Alcatraz.[13]

Alcatraz was new in 1934, and officials wanted to put some famous criminals in it. They chose Capone to be in the first population of prisoners. Capone, who was such a model prisoner that he "obeyed every order the second it was given," was put on the high-security train for Alcatraz.[14]

Because Capone cooperated with the guards and did not join the other prisoners when they did bad things, many of

Alcatraz prison, where Al Capone served part of his sentence, sits upon a rocky island. One of the prison's nicknames is "The Rock."

the other prisoners hated him. They called him "phony Caponi" and several tried to kill him.[15] One prisoner threw a heavy lump of metal at Capone's head, another tried to poison his coffee, another tried to strangle him, and one stabbed him repeatedly with barber shears.[16]

On February 5, 1938, things got even worse. That morning, Capone suddenly started to act odd as if he did not know where he was or what he was doing. The warden asked him after the episode had passed, "What happened to you this morning?" "I dunno, warden," Capone answered. "They tell me I acted like I was a little wacky."[17]

Unfortunately, Capone was more than a little wacky, although there were times when he seemed all right. He had contracted syphilis, a sexually-transmitted disease (STD), years before. The syphilis bacteria had worked their way into his brain. He spent the rest of his time at Alcatraz in what they called a "bug cage," a cell made of hog wire that was in a corridor off the prison hospital.

Capone's wife, Mae, had heard about his problems through newspaper reports. She wanted to travel to Alcatraz immediately, but authorities told her to wait. It was not until August that she and Sonny were able to go see Capone. (Sonny was nineteen and in college.) In one of his clear times afterward, Capone did not mourn his own situation, he mourned his son's: "I tried to keep all this from the kid when he was little. I tried to be a good father. I didn't want him to know about me. Now he comes and sees me here, like this. It must have hit him between the eyes."[18]

In January 1939, Capone's time in Alcatraz was up. Instead of sending him back to the Cook County Jail for the final year, they let him finish up in the Terminal Island correctional facility down the California coast.

Finally, Capone's time at Terminal Island was over (again shortened for good behavior). He was sent back East on a train and released in Pennsylvania on November 16, 1939. Ralph, Mae, and Sonny came to pick him up in a limousine and took him right to a hospital in Baltimore known for its treatment of syphilis.

Although the doctors could give Capone things to kill the syphilis bacterium, they could not fix the damage to his brain. When Chicago reporters asked Jake Guzik whether

Capone would return to head up the outfit again, Guzik said no because "Al is nuttier than a fruitcake."[19]

When Capone's treatment was finished in March 1940, he did not go to Chicago. He went instead to Florida. His mother still lived in the Chicago house, but Mae, Mae's sister, and the sister's husband lived with Capone at his home on Palm Island. Sonny was married on December 30, 1941, to a girl he had met in high school. They lived nearby and had four daughters. Capone loved to play with his granddaughters and gave them presents whenever he could. He could not work anymore, though, so the only money they had was the six hundred dollars that Ralph sent to Mae every week.

On January 19, 1947, only two days after his forty-eighth birthday, Al Capone started to bleed inside his head and it looked like he was going to die. His condition seemed so bad, in fact, that a major news organization even reported that he had died. But he started to get better, which gave the rest of his family time to travel to Miami.

Al Capone eventually fell ill again and died on January 25, 1947. His mother, wife, son, brothers, and sister were all with him when he died. His body was taken to Chicago and, on a frigidly cold February 4, he was buried between his father and his brother Frank.

Here is what happened to some of the other people:

- Sonny was invited to join the outfit, and he needed the money. But when he mentioned it to his mother, Mae said, "Your father broke my heart. Don't you break it." He turned the offer down.

- Capone's mother, Teresa, died in 1952 at the age of eighty-five.

- Capone's wife, Mae, died in Florida on April 16, 1986, when she was eighty-nine years old.

- Ralph Capone was again charged with tax evasion in the 1950s. He paid up without going to court this time, and died November 22, 1974, in Wisconsin, at the age of eighty.

- Frank "The Enforcer" Nitti killed himself in 1943. He was facing another prison term for tax evasion.

- Johnny Torrio, Capone's mentor in crime, was charged with tax evasion, too. Halfway through the trial he changed his plea to guilty and was sentenced to two and a half years in Leavenworth.

- Eliot Ness became more famous after he died than when he was alive. He died of a heart attack May 16, 1957, at age fifty-four, shortly after approving the final draft of his book, *The Untouchables* (written with Oscar Fraley), but before the book was published. A popular television series and several movies were based on Ness's story. The cartoon character, Dick Tracy, was also based on Ness.[20]

Alcatraz Prison became too expensive to run and was shut down in 1963. It became a part of the National Park Service's Golden Gate Recreation Area and is now a tourist attraction.

chapter eight

WHERE ARE WE TODAY?

AFTERMATH—"It's the Al Capone method of law enforcement: If you can't get them on anything else, get them on tax fraud."[1]

Encouraged by the Prohibition-era results, Congress passed tax laws aimed at gambling and trafficking in another illegal substance, marijuana. These tax laws required gamblers or marijuana dealers to file reports of who they were and what they were doing, then required them to pay a special tax.

In the 1960s, people challenged these laws—using the same argument that Manley Sullivan had used back in the 1920s—but this time, they won. In a series of court cases in 1968 and 1969, the Supreme Court decided that the laws *did* violate the gamblers' and marijuana dealers' Fifth Amendment rights because:

- it was clear that Congress intended the laws to catch crooks, not to raise money;

- only people who were likely to be doing illegal things were required to make the filings;

- the forms asked for information that would make it easier to convict the filer for non-tax crimes; and

- law enforcement officers were specifically permitted to look at the information.[2]

In the 1980s, states started to pass tax laws targeted at illegal drugs. Lawmakers tried to write the laws so the Supreme Court would not strike them down. These laws are known as Al Capone laws.[3]

Meanwhile, the government still prosecutes income tax evasion. The Special Intelligence Unit headed by Elmer Irey has become the IRS's Criminal Investigation Division (CID). When Irey headed it, the SIU only investigated violations of the Internal Revenue Code. But the unit was so good at it that, over the years, Congress expanded their responsibilities to include other kinds of crimes involving money and banks. The SIU was started with six men; the CID now has about three thousand agents.[4]

The Criminal Investigation Division has several programs, some of them aimed at the same things Irey was aiming for.

General Tax Fraud

In the mid- to late-1990s, CID's General Fraud Program resulted in the conviction of about one thousand people each year for tax fraud; about 70 percent of them went to jail. The average prison sentence was a little less than two years.[5]

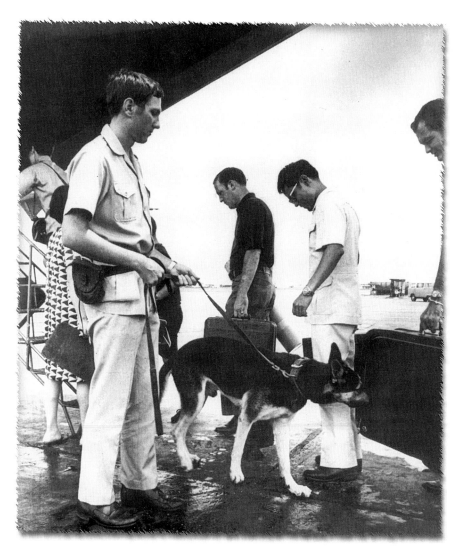

Dogs are still used to find illegal substances. During Prohibition, they searched for alcohol, now they find illegal drugs.

Public Corruption

Corruption of public officials still exists, and the CID has a program to combat that, too. In the mid- to late-1990s, CID's Public Corruption Program saw the conviction of about one hundred corrupt officials each year. More of them went to jail than the "general" category, but the average jail sentence was about the same.[6]

Organized Crime

In the mid- to late-1990s, CID's Organized Crime Program saw the conviction of between 150 to 250 gangsters per year. Around 80 percent of those convicted were sent to jail. The average jail sentence for gangsters was about twice as long as the average jail sentence for corrupt officials or general fraud.[7] This program battles organizations like the group that Al Capone headed. John Gotti is thought to be head of the Gambino crime family in New York. He was sentenced in September 1999 to six years and five months in prison after he pleaded guilty to doing the same thing Ralph Capone did—reporting too little income on his income tax return. (He pleaded guilty to some other things, too.)

But there is controversy. There are those who say it is wrong to use tax laws (meant to raise money) in order to convict people who may have committed other crimes.

Other people say they do not mind if someone goes to jail for tax evasion if that is what he or she did. But they worry that if the government is really trying to jail someone for other reasons, then the courts may be tempted to convict

People are still trying to find creative ways to transport illegal substances. This man has tied illegal drugs to his legs.

someone for tax evasion without requiring the prosecution to really prove its case.

On the other hand, there are people who say, "Let's not lose sight of what's really going on here. In Capone's case, this guy was *known* to have murdered people and to be running all kinds of illegal enterprises. The reason officials could not convict him on those charges was because he had corrupted the police and scared everybody else. *Any* way to get this guy—and other people like him—sent away to prison is a good way and good for society."

What do you think?

Questions for Discussion

1. If it is wrong to make money from illegal activities, should the federal government be able to make money by taxing people who engage in illegal activities? Explain your answer.

2. If honest people have to pay taxes on their income, why should dishonest people be excused from paying taxes? If only the honest are taxed, is that like a punishment for honesty? Explain your answer.

3. If people have made money from doing bad things, why can't the government take some of the money away and use it for good things? Does it make sense for the government to tax illegal income and use the taxes to pay for things like medical research and food for hungry people? Explain your answer.

4. Al Capone set up a soup kitchen so that many people who could not buy food during the Depression could get a free meal. Some say he did it because he really cared about the people. Others say he did not care about the people, he only did it to get good publicity. Were Capone's motives important, or was the fact that hungry people got fed good enough? Explain your answer.

Chapter Notes

Chapter 1. Massacre

1. John Kobler, *Capone: The Life and World of Al Capone* (New York: G.P. Putnam's Sons, 1971), p. 252.

2. Laurence Bergreen, *Capone: The Man and the Era* (New York: Simon & Schuster, 1994), p. 312.

3. Robert J. Schoenberg, *Mr. Capone* (New York: William Morrow & Company, Inc., 1992), p. 214.

4. Kobler, p. 250.

5. Bergreen, p. 307.

6. Kobler, p. 253.

7. Schoenberg, p. 159.

8. Kobler, p. 87.

9. Ibid., p. 171.

10. Paul W. Heimel, *Eliot Ness: The Real Story* (Coudersport, Pa.: Knox Books, 1997), p. 51.

Chapter 2. Al Capone

1. Laurence Bergreen, *Capone: The Man and the Era* (New York: Simon & Schuster, 1994), p. 27; John Kobler, *Capone: The Life and World of Al Capone* (New York: G. P. Putnam's Sons, 1971), p. 18.

2. Kobler, p. 17.

3. Ibid., p. 24.

4. Kobler, p. 18.

5. Rick Hornung, *Al Capone* (New York: Random House Inc., 1998), p. 10.

6. Bergreen, p. 38.

7. Robert J. Schoenberg, *Mr. Capone* (New York: William Morrow & Company, Inc., 1992), p. 46.

8. Kobler, p. 66.

9. Bergreen, p. 236.

10. Elmer L. Irey as told to William J. Slocum, *The Tax Dodgers* (New York: Greenberg, 1948), p. 44.

11. Bergreen, p. 149.

12. Hornung, p. 50.

13. Schoenberg, p. 175.

14. Ibid., pp. 45, 177.

15. Ibid., p. 179.

16. Ibid., p. 204.

17. Kobler, p. 14.

18. Bergreen, p. 295.

19. Schoenberg, p. 138.

20. Bergreen, p. 138.

21. Timothy Jacobs, *The Gangsters* (Hong Kong: Mallard Press, 1990), p. 32.

22. Schoenberg, p. 204.

23. Ibid., p. 206.

24. Bergreen, p. 216.

25. Ibid., p. 207.

26. Kobler, p. 236.

27. Schoenberg, pp. 188–189.

28. Ibid., p. 182.

29. Kobler, p. 215.

30. Bergreen, p. 16.

Chapter 3. Life in the Days of Al Capone

1. Library of Congress, image # LC-USZ62-17081, Washington, D.C. (1879).

2. Robert J. Schoenberg, *Mr. Capone* (New York: William Morrow & Company, Inc., 1992), p. 56.

3. United States Constitution, Eighteenth Amendment.

4. *Our Century: 1920–1930* (Milwaukee: Gareth Stevens Publishing, 1993), p. 42.

5. *This Fabulous Century: 1920–1930* (New York: Time-Life Books, 1969), vol. 3, pp. 164–165.

6. Schoenberg, p. 110.

7. Ralph K. Andrist, ed., *The American Heritage History of the 20s and 30s* (New York: American Heritage Publishing Co., Inc., 1970), p. 83.

8. Elmer L. Irey as told to William J. Slocum, *The Tax Dodgers* (New York: Greenberg, 1948), pp. 5–6.

9. Ibid., p. 6.

10. Schoenberg, p. 181.

11. John Kobler, *Capone: The Life and World of Al Capone* (New York: G.P. Putnam's Sons, 1971), p. 141.

12. Laurence Bergreen, *Capone: The Man and the Era* (New York: Simon & Schuster, 1994), p. 277.

13. Schoenberg, p. 176.

14. Paul W. Heimel, *Eliot Ness: The Real Story* (Coudersport, Pa.: Knox Books, 1997), p. 107.

15. *Pollock* v. *Farmers' Loan & Trust Co.*, 157 U.S. 429 (1895).

16. *Brushaber* v. *Union Pacific Railroad Company*, 240 U.S. 1 (1916).

17. *United States* v. *Sullivan*, 274 U.S. 259 (1927).

18. Ibid., p. 263.

Chapter 4. The Road to Court

1. Paul W. Heimel, *Eliot Ness: The Real Story* (Coudersport, Pa.: Knox Books, 1997), p. 17.

2. Eliot Ness and Oscar Fraley, *The Untouchables* (Cutchogue, N.Y.: Buccaneer Books, Inc., 1993), p. 21.

3. Ibid.

4. Ibid., p. 22.

5. Ibid.

6. Heimel, p. 83.

7. Ness and Fraley, p. 145.

8. Ibid., p. 185.

9. Ibid., pp. 185–186.

10. Ibid., pp. 203–204.

11. Ibid., pp. 208–209.

12. Heimel, p. 115.

13. Elmer L. Irey as told to William J. Slocum, *The Tax Dodgers* (New York: Greenberg, 1948), p. x.

14. *O'Brien* v. *United States*, 51F(2d) 193, 197 (1931).

15. Ibid.

16. Ibid., p. 195.

17. Ibid.

18. Irey as told to Slocum, p. 28.

19. Ibid., p. 30.

20. Robert J. Schoenberg, *Mr. Capone* (New York: William Morrow & Company, Inc., 1992), p. 243.

21. John Kobler, *Capone: The Life and World of Al Capone* (New York: G. P. Putnam's Sons, 1971), p. 282.

22. Irey as told to Slocum, p. 48.

23. Schoenberg, p. 248.

24. Ibid., p. 300.

25. Ibid., p. 256.

Chapter 5. The Court

1. Robert J. Schoenberg, *Mr. Capone* (New York: William Morrow & Company, Inc., 1992), p. 311.

2. Elmer L. Irey as told to William J. Slocum, *The Tax Dodgers* (New York: Greenberg, 1948), p. 61.

3. Schoenberg, p. 314.

4. Rick Hornung, *Al Capone* (New York: Random House, Inc., 1998), p. 154.

5. Irey as told to Slocum, p. 62.

6. Schoenberg, p. 316.

7. John Kobler, *Capone: The Life and World of Al Capone* (New York: G.P. Putnam's Sons, 1971), p. 343.

8. Ibid.

9. Schoenberg, p. 319.

10. Ibid., p. 321.

11. Ibid., p. 323.

Chapter 6. The Decision

1. Laurence Bergreen, *Capone: The Man and the Era* (New York: Simon & Schuster, 1994), p. 484.

2. John Kobler, *Capone: The Life and World of Al Capone* (New York: G.P. Putnam's Sons, 1971), p. 350.

Chapter 7. The Aftermath

1. *Capone v. United States*, 56 F (2d) 927 (1932).

2. *Capone v. United States*, 286 U.S. 553 (1932).

3. Laurence Bergreen, *Capone: The Man and the Era* (New York: Simon & Schuster, 1994), p. 498.

4. Ibid., p. 500.

5. Eliot Ness and Oscar Fraley, *The Untouchables* (Cutchogue, N.Y.: Buccaneer Books, Inc., 1993), p. 252.

6. Ibid., p. 253.

7. *United States v. Scharton*, 285 U.S. 518 (1932).

8. *Capone v. Alderhold*, 2 FSupp. 280, 282 (1933).

9. *Capone v. Alderhold*, 293 U.S. 598 (1934).

10. Robert J. Schoenberg, *Mr. Capone* (New York: William Morrow & Company, Inc., 1992), p. 329.

11. Bergreen, p. 517.

12. Ibid., p. 543.

13. John Kobler, *Capone: The Life and World of Al Capone* (New York: G.P. Putnam's Sons, 1971), p. 369.

14. The National Park Service, "Alcatraz Island—U.S. Penitentiary," <http://www.nps.gov/alcatraz/pen2.html> (March 23, 2001).

15. Rick Hornung, *Al Capone* (New York: Random House, Inc., 1998), p. 163.

16. Schoenberg, p. 340; Kobler, p. 375.

17. Bergreen, p. 559.

18. Ibid., p. 563.

19. Kobler, p. 381.

20. Bergreen, p. 529.

Chapter 8. Where Are We Today?

1. Christopher Paul Sorrow, "The New Al Capone Laws and the Double Jeopardy Implications of Taxing Illegal Drugs," *Southern California Interdisciplinary Law Journal*, vol. 4, 1995, p. 323.

2. *Leary* v. *United States*, 395 U.S. 6 (1969).

3. Sorrow, p. 323.

4. Department of the Treasury, "Criminal Investigation Division Annual Report," © 1998, <http://www.treas.gov/irs/ci/annual_report/progbk98.htm#publiccorruption> (March 23, 2001).

5. Department of the Treasury, "Criminal Investigation Division Annual Report—General Fraud" © 1998, <http://www.treas.gov/irs/ci/annual_report/graphs/general.gif> (March 23, 2001).

6. Department of the Treasury, "Criminal Investigation Division Annual Report—General Fraud" © 1998, <http://www.treas.gov/irs/ci/annual_report/graphs/pc.gif> (March 23, 2001).

7. Department of the Treasury, "Criminal Investigation Division Annual Report—General Fraud" © 1998, <http://www.treas.gov/irs/ci/annual_report/graphs/oc.gif> (March 23, 2001).

Glossary

bootlegging—Illegally making, transporting, and/or selling alcoholic beverages.

corrupt, corruption—When public officials do not do their job fairly, but accept money to do special favors. The money given to a public official in return for a special favor is called a "bribe."

count—A specific criminal charge. One of Capone's indictments contained several claims of tax crimes for the years 1925–1929. Each separate claim is a "count;" that indictment had twenty-two counts. The counts define what the prosecutor has to prove.

deduction—An expense that the law lets taxpayers subtract from their income before figuring out income tax. There are deductions for business expenses, childcare expenses, and charitable contributions. Anything the law allows to be subtracted is called "deductible." Generally speaking, the more that can be deducted, the less income tax will be paid. Gambling losses are deductible from gambling income.

felony—The general word for a really serious crime. Felonies generally carry severe punishments like long prison sentences. Tax evasion is a felony. A person guilty of a felony is a "felon."

grand jury—A group of people that decides whether there will be a criminal trial. The prosecutor presents evidence to a grand jury to try to show there is reason to believe that a specific person did specific crime(s). If the grand jury thinks there is a good chance that the person did the crime, it issues an indictment.

income tax—A tax based on how much money a person makes. When people talk about the income tax, they usually mean the *federal* income tax collected by the IRS, although some states have income taxes, too.

indictment—A formal charge against someone. An indictment does not mean that person is guilty; it says there seems to be enough evidence to warrant a trial.

Internal Revenue Service (IRS)—This is the federal agency that collects federal income taxes. At the time of the Capone trial, it was called the Bureau of Internal Revenue.

misdemeanor—A minor crime that is not as bad as a felony. It carries a shorter jail sentence than a felony. Failure to file a tax return is a misdemeanor.

organized crime—A group that pursues criminal activity. Like other organizations, a) it has a leader, b) it assigns members to different roles, including supervising other members, and c) it disciplines members that get out of line. What makes organized crime different from legal organizations is that some or all of its business(es) are illegal, and the way they discipline members is sometimes illegal, too.

plea bargain—A deal that the accused party in a trial makes to agree to lesser charges.

Prohibition—The fourteen years from January 1920 to December 1933 when it was illegal to make, transport, or sell alcoholic beverages in the United States.

prosecute, prosecutor—To try to prove in court that someone is guilty of a crime. The government lawyer who does this is called a prosecutor. (Only government lawyers can prosecute someone for a crime; private citizens cannot.)

racket; racketeer, racketeering—A way of getting money from people by force or by cheating. It is thought that this word came from a practice in New York years ago where neighborhood bullies would give a party and make people buy tickets to it—or else. A person who engages in rackets is a "racketeer." To make money through rackets is called "racketeering."

statute of limitations—A limited time period, starting with the date something happened, for bringing a lawsuit. After that time is up, nobody can sue.

tax—An amount of money that the government requires people to pay so that the government can have income. Income taxes are not the only kind of tax. Other kinds of taxes include property tax, service tax, and sales tax.

taxable income—The portion of people's income that is taxed—after they subtract allowable deductions and exclusions.

tax avoidance—Playing by the rules to reduce the amount of income tax paid to the government. This is legal.

tax evasion—Cheating in order to reduce the amount of income tax paid. This is a crime.

tax return—The forms that people send to the IRS every year to show how much they owe or how much they are owed. If any money is owed, it must be sent with the return form.

temperance—The term for not drinking alcoholic beverages.

Further Reading

Cozic, Charles P., ed. *Opposing Viewpoints: Gangs.* San Diego: Greenhaven Press, Inc., 1996.

Hill, Prescott. *Our Century: 1920-1930.* Milwaukee: Gareth Stevens Publishing, 1993.

Jacobs, Timothy. *The Gangsters.* Hong Kong: Mallard Press, 1990.

Nash, Jay Robert. *Bloodletters and Badmen.* New York: M. Evans and Company, Inc., 1995.

Sharman, Margaret. *1920s.* Austin, Tex.: Raintree Steck-Vaughn Publishers, 1993.

Stockdale, Tom. *The Life and Times of Al Capone.* Philadelphia: Chelsea House Publishers, 1998.

Internet Addresses

Federal Bureau of Investigations (FBI) Famous Cases: Al Capone

<http://www.fbi.gov/libref/historic/famcases/capone/capone.htm>

DiscoverySchool.com A–Z History
Al Capone

<http://school.discovery.com/homeworkhelp/worldbook/atozhistory/c/093700.html>

National Archives and Records Administration
Al Capone

<http://www.archives.gov/exhibit_hall/american_originals/capone.html>

Index